ENGLISH TOWN

FOR EVERYONE

STARTER

Contents

Characters

Theme Song

Hello Song

Hello, everyone.
Hello, teacher!
Hello, friends!

Let's have fun together.
We'll have a good time.

Are you ready to start?
We're ready!

Here we go!

Goodbye Song

Did you have fun?

It's time to say goodbye.
See you next time!
See you next time!

Did you enjoy the class?
Yes! We had a fun time!
Yes! We had a fun time!

See you later! See you later!
Goodbye. Goodbye.

Bye! Bye!

Lesson 1 First Day at School

Talk 1

A. Look, listen, and repeat.

Hello, everyone.
I'm Rina Johns.

Hello, Ms. Johns.

Hello. I'm Rina Johns.

Hello, Ms. Johns.

B. Listen, match, and say.

1

2

Talk 2

A. Listen and sing.

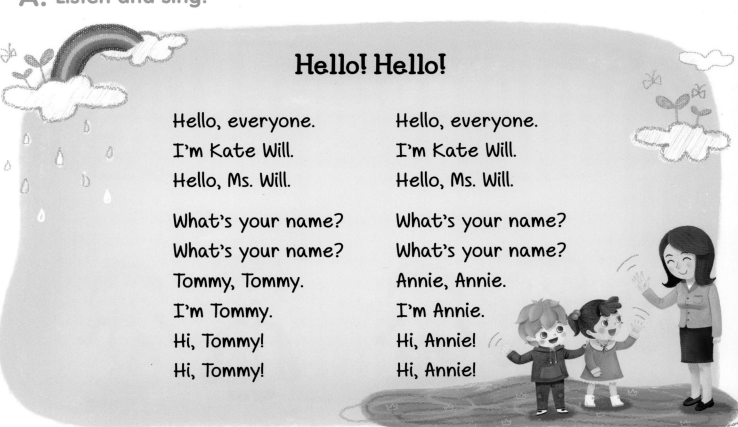

Hello! Hello!

Hello, everyone.
I'm Kate Will.
Hello, Ms. Will.

What's your name?
What's your name?
Tommy, Tommy.
I'm Tommy.
Hi, Tommy!
Hi, Tommy!

Hello, everyone.
I'm Kate Will.
Hello, Ms. Will.

What's your name?
What's your name?
Annie, Annie.
I'm Annie.
Hi, Annie!
Hi, Annie!

B. Look, listen, and repeat. 

What's your name?

I'm Amy.

What's your name?

I'm Amy.

e-learning

C. Listen and point. Make sentences.

I'm ________.

1

Mark

2

Jenny

3

Tylor

4

Amy

A: What's your name?
B: I'm ________.

D. Listen, point, and say.

1 Mark

2 Amy

3 Tylor

4 Jenny

Lesson 2 Greetings

Talk 1

A. Look, listen, and repeat.

Nice to meet you.

Nice to meet you, too.

Nice to meet you.

Nice to meet you, too.

B. Listen, check, and say.

1 ⓐ

☐

ⓑ

☐

2 ⓐ

☐

ⓑ

☐

Talk 2

A. Listen and sing.

Nice to Meet You

Nice to meet you.
Nice to meet you, too.

How are you today?
How are you today?
Good. Good.
Good. Good.

Nice to meet you.
Nice to meet you, too.

How are you today?
How are you today?
Great. Great.
Great. Great.

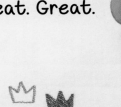

B. Look, listen, and repeat. 

How are you today?

Good.

How are you today?

Good.

e-learning

C. Listen and say.

1

Good.

2

Not so good.

3

Great.

4

Bad.

A: How are you today?
B: ________

D. Listen, point, and say.

1 2 3 4

Alphabet Phonics Aa~Dd

Phonics Time 

A. Look, listen, and repeat.

A	B	C	D	E	F	G	H	I	J	K	L	M	N	O	P	Q	R	S	T	U	V	W	X	Y	Z
a	b	c	d	e	f	g	h	i	j	k	l	m	n	o	p	q	r	s	t	u	v	w	x	y	z

B. Listen and chant.

A	says a, a, a	a, a, ant	a, a, apple		
B	says b, b, b	b, b, ball	b, b, bear		
C	says c, c, c	c, c, cake	c, c, cat		
D	says d, d, d	d, d, dog	d, d, doll		

C. Find and circle. Read along.

The ant likes the apple.
The bear likes the ball.
The cat likes the cake.
The dog likes the doll.

Fun Time
Start
1 A: Hello. I'm Tom.
B: ________
6 Let's sing on page 7.
7 A: How are you today?
B: ________
8 Hello.
Mark
9 I'm Mark.
I'm Jenny.
10 Next time!
Finish
15 A: ________?
B: I'm Amy.

Golden Gate Bridge
Go 1. Go 2. Go 3.
2 Nice to meet you.
3 Next time!
LONDON SIGHTSEEING
5 Great!
4
A: What's your name?
B: I'm ________.
Tim
11 Let's sing on page 11.
12 Return to Start!
13 A: Nice to meet you.
B: ________________
14 Not so good.

Classroom

Talk 1

A. Look, listen, and repeat.

Yes, it is.

Is this a pencil case?

Is this a pencil case?

No, it isn't.

B. Listen, circle, and say.

ⓐ

2 ⓐ

ⓑ

Talk 2

A. Listen and sing.

Is This a Pencil Case?

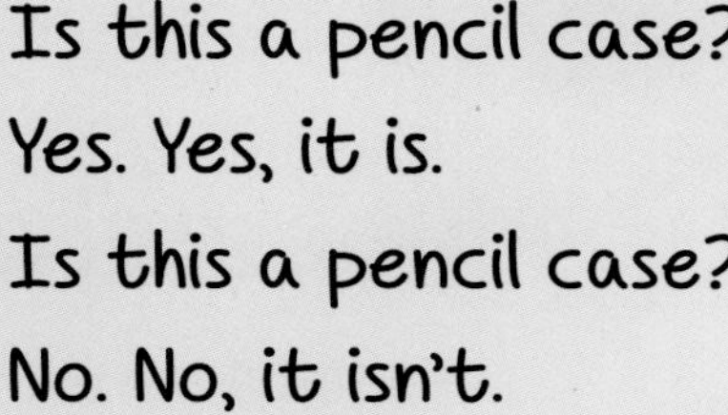

Is this a pencil case?
Yes. Yes, it is.
Is this a pencil case?
No. No, it isn't.

What's this? What's this?
A blackboard. A blackboard.
It's a blackboard.

What's this? What's this?
A computer. A computer.
It's a computer.

B. Look, listen, and repeat.

What's this?

It's a blackboard.

Say and Act

What's this?

It's a blackboard.

e-learning

C. Listen and point. Make sentences.

It's a ________.

1

blackboard

2

computer

desk

4

television

D. Listen, point, and say.

A: What's this?
B: It's a ________.

1 2 3 4

Lesson 5 Toys

Talk 1

A. Look, listen, and repeat.

Let's play.

Okay.

Let's play.

Okay.

B. Listen, match, and say.

1

2

Is this a pencil?

Talk 2

A. Listen and sing.

What's That?

What's that?
What's that?
What's that?
It's a yo-yo.
It's a yo-yo.

Let's play! Let's play!
Okay. Okay.

What's that?
What's that?
What's that?
It's a ball.
It's a ball.

Let's play! Let's play!
Okay. Okay.

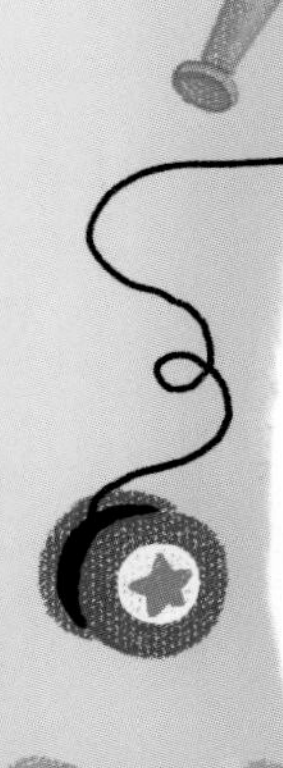

B. Look, listen, and repeat. 

What's that?

It's a yo-yo.

Say and Act

What's that?

It's a yo-yo.

e-learning

C. Listen and point. Make sentences.

It's a ________.

1 ball

2 bat

3 jump rope

4 yo-yo

A: What's that?
B: It's a ________.

D. Listen, point, and say.

Lesson 6 Alphabet Phonics Ee~Hh

Phonics Time

A. Look, listen, and repeat.

A	B	C	D	E	F	G	H	I	J	K	L	M	N	O	P	Q	R	S	T	U	V	W	X	Y	Z
a	b	c	d	e	f	g	h	i	j	k	l	m	n	o	p	q	r	s	t	u	v	w	x	y	z

e-learning

B. Listen and chant.

E says e, e, e e, e, egg e, e, elephant  

F says f, f, f f, f, farm f, f, fox  

G says g, g, g g, g, goat g, g, goose  

H says h, h, h h, h, horse h, h, house  

C. Find and circle. Read along.

The elephant has an egg.
The fox plays on the farm.
The goose plays with the goat.
The horse is in the house.

Fun Time
Start
1 A: What's this?
B: ____________
2 It's a computer.
3 Next time!
4 Let's sing on page 19.
5 It's a desk.
It's a pencil case.
6
What's this?
7 A: ____________?
B: It's a yo-yo.
8 A: Is this a ball?
B: ____________

Go 1. Go 2. Go 3.
12 blackboard
11 Go ahead 4.
13 Next time!
10 A: Let's play.
B: Okay.
14 Let's sing on page 23.
9 Return to Start!
15 It's a bat.
Finish
16 Let's play ______.

Lesson 7 Colors

Talk 1

A. Look, listen, and repeat.

Sit down, please.

Sure.

Sit down, please.

Sure.

B. Listen, check, and say.

1 a

b

2 a

b

Talk 2

A. Listen and sing.

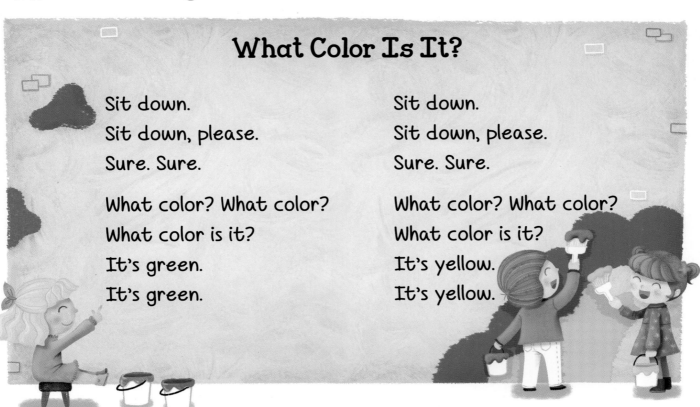

What Color Is It?

Sit down.
Sit down, please.
Sure. Sure.

What color? What color?
What color is it?
It's green.
It's green.

Sit down.
Sit down, please.
Sure. Sure.

What color? What color?
What color is it?
It's yellow.
It's yellow.

B. Look, listen, and repeat.

What color is it?

It's green.

Say and Act

What color is it?

It's green.

e-learning

C. Listen and point. Make sentences.

It's ________.

1 blue

2 green

3 red

4 yellow

D. Listen, point, and say.

A: What color is it?
B: It's ________.

Lesson 8 Shapes

Talk 1

A. Look, listen, and repeat.

Oops, I'm sorry.

That's okay.

Oops, I'm sorry.

That's okay.

B. Listen, circle, and say.

1 ⓐ

ⓑ

2 ⓐ

ⓑ

Talk 2

A. Listen and sing.

Draw a Star

Oops, oops, I'm sorry.
I'm sorry. I'm sorry.
Okay, okay.
That's okay.
That's okay.
That's okay.

A star, a star.
Draw a star.
Okay. Okay.

A circle, a circle.
Draw a circle.
Okay. Okay.

B. Look, listen, and repeat.

Draw a star.

Okay.

Draw a star.

Okay.

e-learning

C. Listen and point. Make sentences.

Draw a ________.

1 circle

2 square

3 star

4 triangle

D. Listen, point, and say.

A: Draw a ________.
B: Okay.

Alphabet Phonics Ii~Ll

Phonics Time

A. Look, listen, and repeat.

A	B	C	D	E	F	G	H	I	J	K	L	M	N	O	P	Q	R	S	T	U	V	W	X	Y	Z
a	b	c	d	e	f	g	h	i	j	k	l	m	n	o	p	q	r	s	t	u	v	w	x	y	z

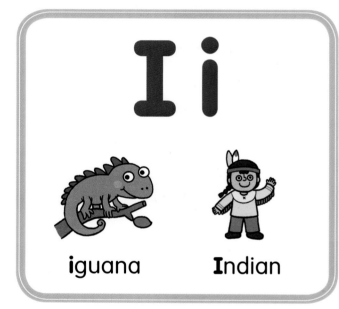

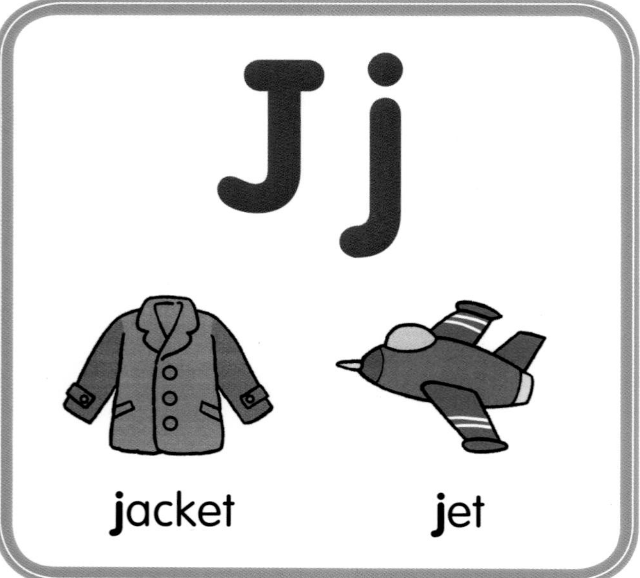

e-learning

B. Listen and chant.

I	says i, i, i	i, i, iguana	i, i, Indian		
J	says j, j, j	j, j, jacket	j, j, jet		
K	says k, k, k	k, k, king	k, k, kite		
L	says l, l, l	l, l, lemon	l, l, lion	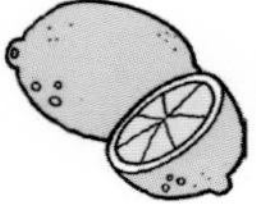	

C. Find and circle. Read along.

The Indian plays with the iguana.
The jacket is on the jet.
The king flies a kite.
The lion licks a lemon.

Fun Time
Start
1 A: What color is it?
B: ________
2 Sit down, please.
14 Sure.
15 A: Draw a triangle.
B: ________
13 star
square
12 Return to Start!
11 Let's sing on page 35.
10 Next time!

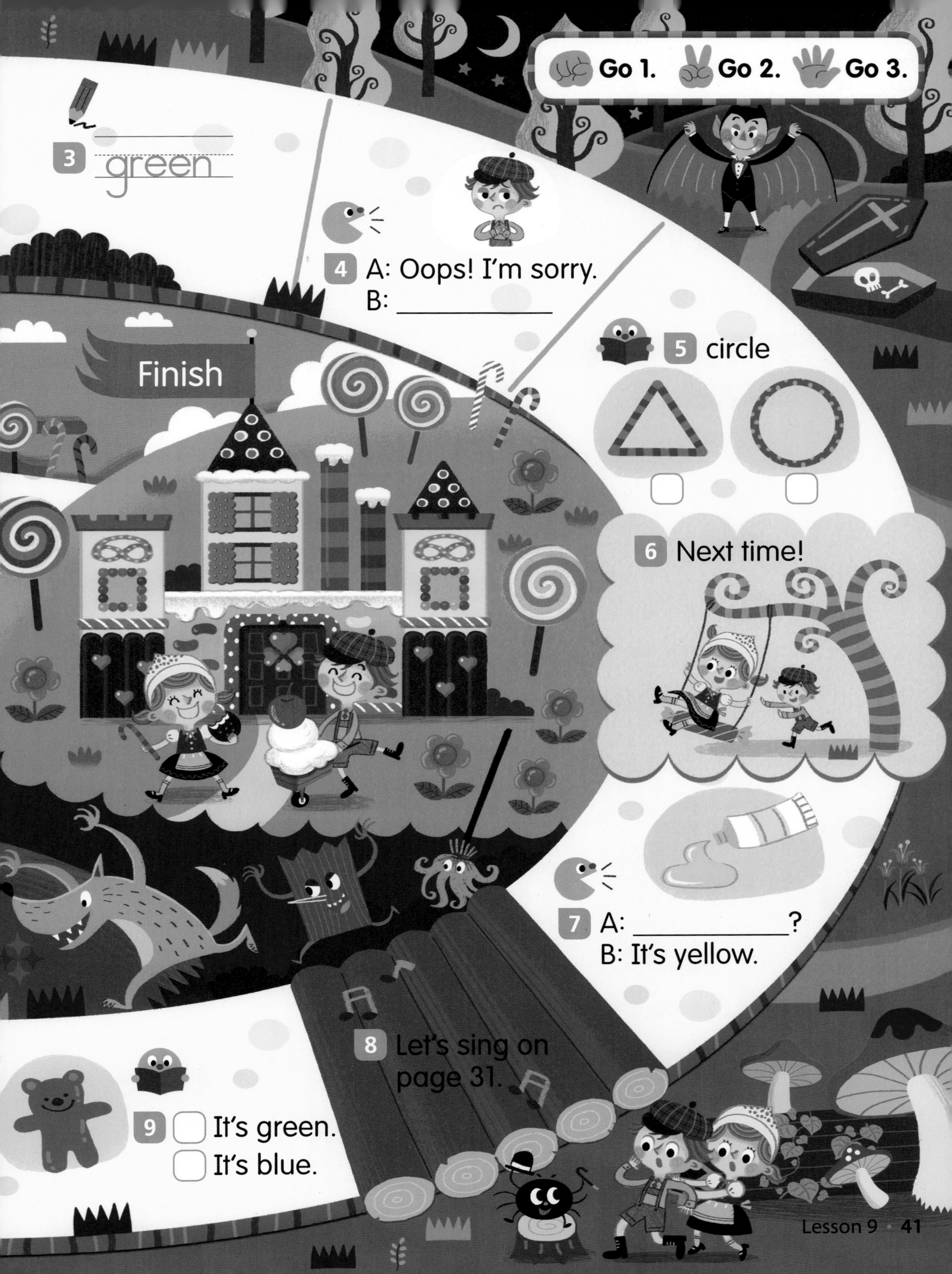
Go 1. Go 2. Go 3.
3 green
4 A: Oops! I'm sorry.
B: ____________
Finish
5 circle
6 Next time!
7 A: ____________?
B: It's yellow.
8 Let's sing on page 31.
9 It's green.
It's blue.

Lesson 10

Assessment Test 1

Listening

A. Listen and check.

1

2

3

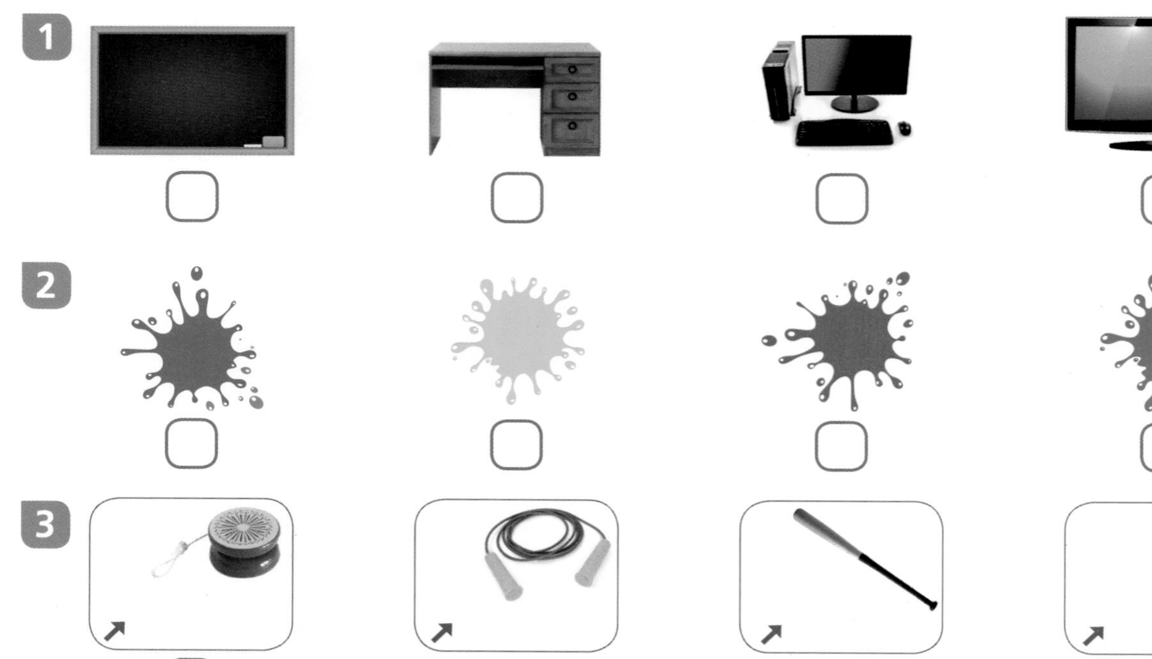

B. Listen and choose O or X.

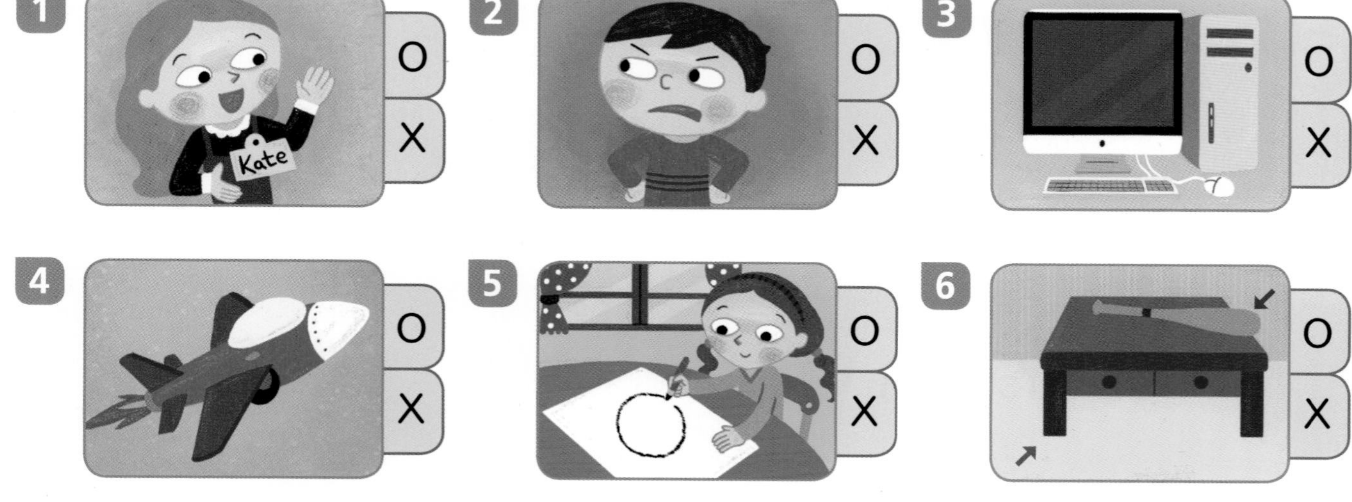

C. Listen and circle.

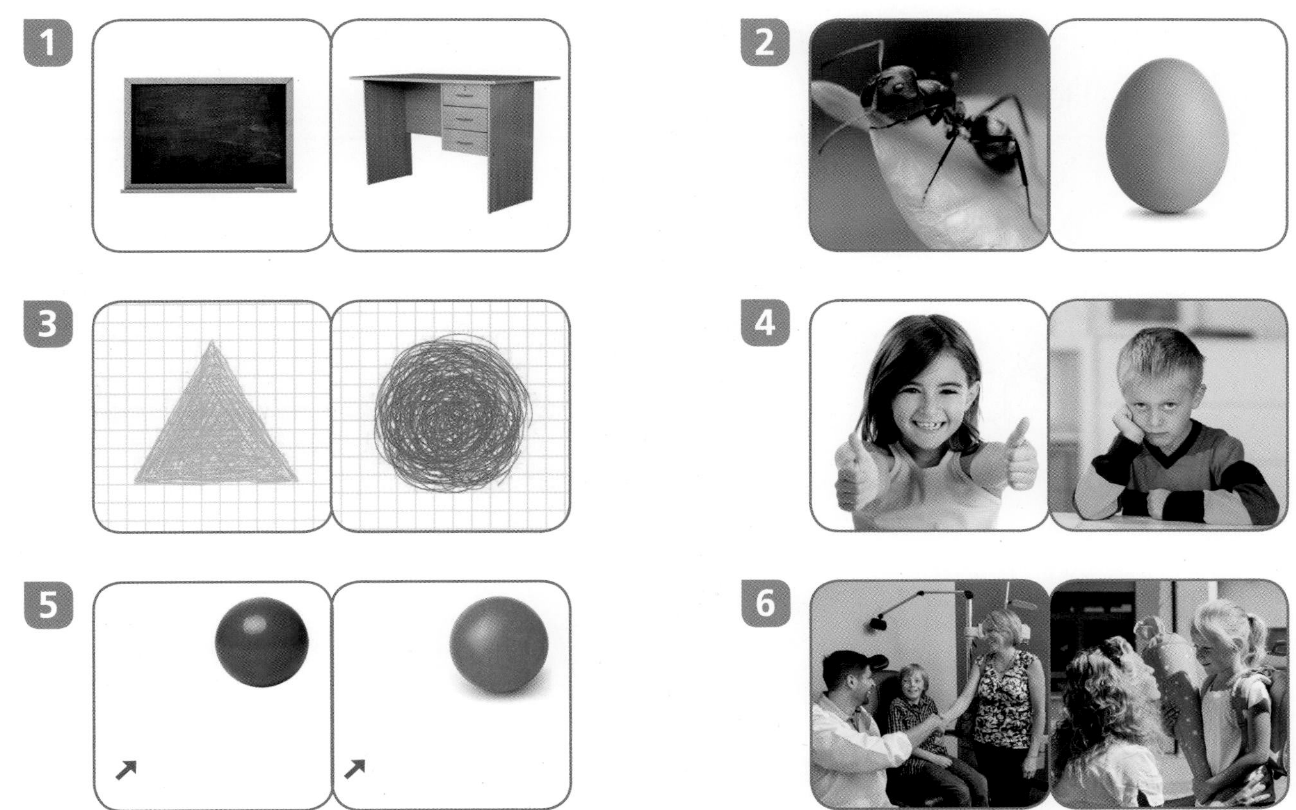

D. Listen and match.

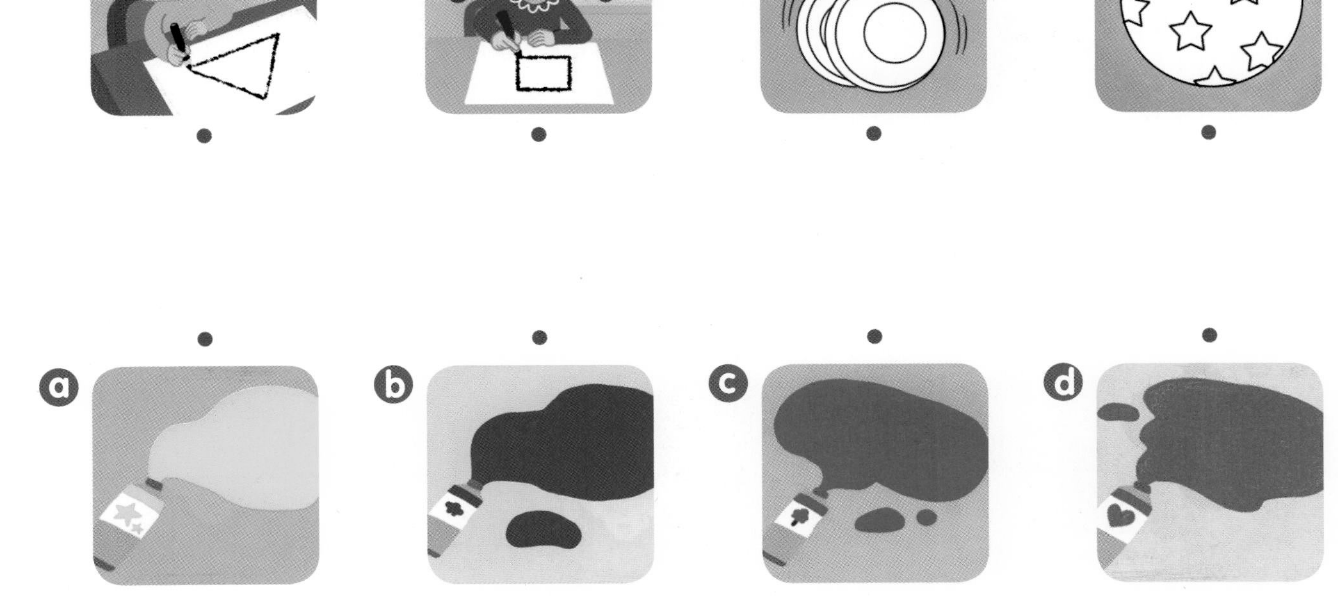

Reading Read and number.

1. Let's play.
2. It's a blue jump rope.
3. It's a yellow iguana.
4. Sit down, please.
5. Hello. I'm Ken.
6. Bad.

Writing Match and trace.

1 

2 

3 

4 

- Draw a kite.
- It's a computer.
- What's your name?
- How are you today?

Speaking

e-learning

A. Look, listen, and answer.

B. Listen and answer.

1

2

3

4

Lesson 11 More Shapes

Talk 1

A. Look, listen, and repeat.

What color is the traffic light?

It's red. Stop!

What color is the traffic light?

It's red. Stop!

B. Listen, number, and say.

Talk 2

A. Listen and sing.

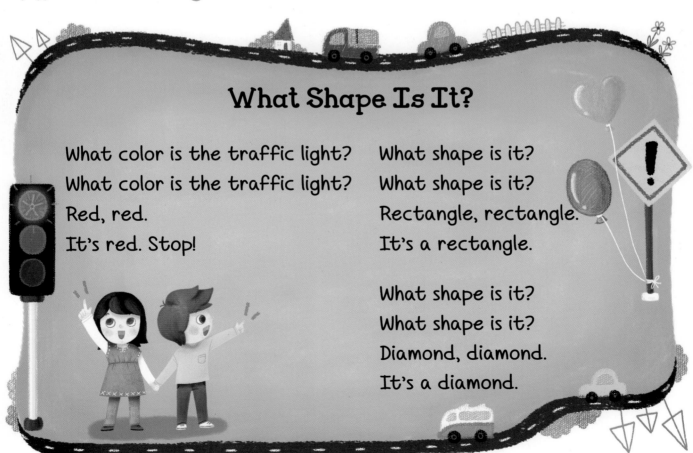

What Shape Is It?

What color is the traffic light?
What color is the traffic light?
Red, red.
It's red. Stop!

What shape is it?
What shape is it?
Rectangle, rectangle.
It's a rectangle.

What shape is it?
What shape is it?
Diamond, diamond.
It's a diamond.

B. Look, listen, and repeat. 

What shape is it?

It's a rectangle.

Say and Act

What shape is it?

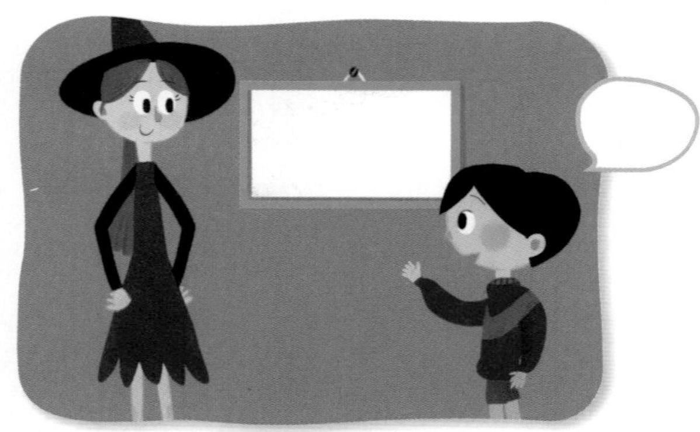

It's a rectangle.

e-learning

C. Listen and point. Make sentences.

It's ________.

1

a diamond

2

a heart

3

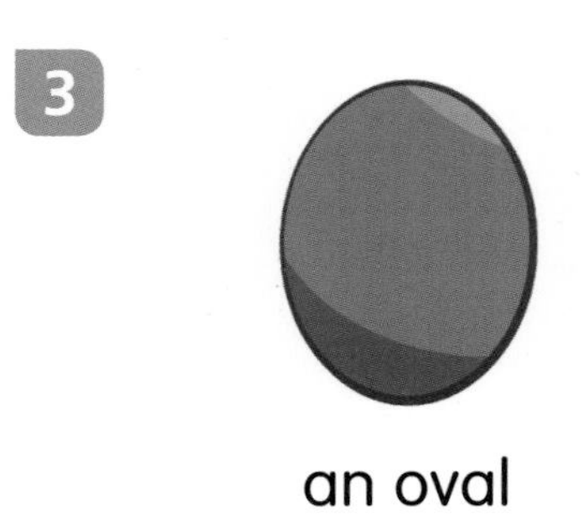

an oval

4

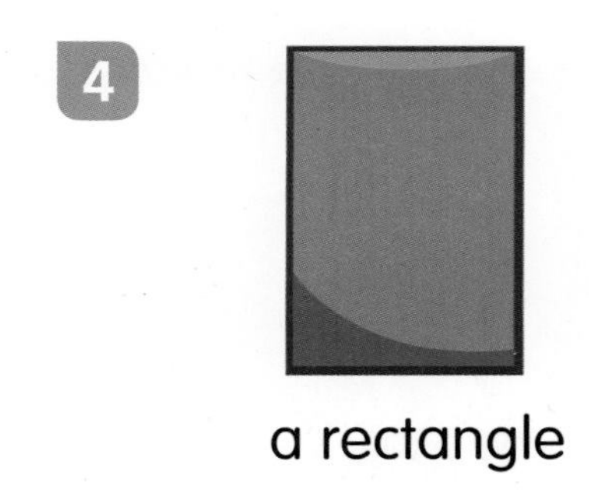

a rectangle

D. Listen, point, and say.

A: What shape is it?
B: It's ________.

1 2 3 4

Lesson 12 House

Talk 1

A. Look, listen, and repeat.

Here you are.

Thank you.

Here you are.

Thank you.

B. Listen, match, and say.

1

2

Talk 2

A. Listen and sing.

Here You Are

Here you are.
Thank you.

Door, door?
Is it a door?
Is it a door?
Yes, yes, yes.
Yes, it is.

Here you are.
Thank you.

Window, window?
Is it a window?
Is it a window?
Yes, yes, yes.
Yes, it is.

B. Look, listen, and repeat. 

Is it a door?

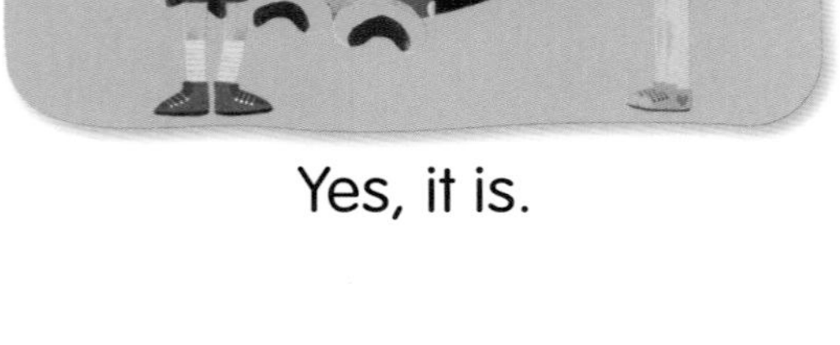

Yes, it is.

Is it a door?

Yes, it is.

e-learning

C. Listen and point. Make sentences.

Is it a ________?

1

chimney

2

door

3

roof

4

window

A: Is it a ________?
B: Yes, it is.

D. Listen, point, and say.

1 2 3 4

Alphabet Phonics Mm~Pp

Phonics Time

A. Look, listen, and repeat.

A	B	C	D	E	F	G	H	I	J	K	L	M	N	O	P	Q	R	S	T	U	V	W	X	Y	Z
a	b	c	d	e	f	g	h	i	j	k	l	m	n	o	p	q	r	s	t	u	v	w	x	y	z

B. Listen and chant.

M	says m, m, m	m, m, man	m, m, milk		
N	says n, n, n	n, n, nurse	n, n, nuts		
O	says o, o, o	o, o, octopus	o, o, ox		
P	says p, p, p	p, p, pig	p, p, pizza		

C. Find and circle. Read along.

The man drinks milk.
The nurse eats nuts.
The ox likes the octopus.
The pig likes pizza.

Fun Time

10
A: What shape is it?
B: ______________
11 Return to Start!
12 It's a rectangle.
It's an oval.
Finish
13 Let's sing on page 51.
14 heart
15 Next time!
STOP
Start
1 A: What color is the traffic light?
B: ________ Stop!
2
Here you are.

Go 1. Go 2. Go 3.
9
A: ________
B: Thank you.
8 It's a window.
18 Is it a chimney?
17 A: ________?
B: Yes, it is.
7
A: Is it a door?
B: ________
6 Go ahead 3.
16 What shape is it?
5 Thank you.
4 Next time!
3 Let's sing on page 47.

 **Talk 1** 

A. Look, listen, and repeat.

Are you hungry?

Yes, I am.

Are you hungry?

No, I'm not.

B. Listen, check, and say.

1 a

b

2 a

b

Talk 2

A. Listen and sing.

Are You Hungry?

Are you hungry?
Are you hungry?
Yes, I am. Yes, I am.

Do you like cookies?
Cookies, cookies.
Yes, I do. Yes, I do.

Are you hungry?
Are you hungry?
No, I'm not. No, I'm not.

Do you like candies?
Candies, candies.
Yes, I do. Yes, I do.

B. Look, listen, and repeat. 

Do you like cookies?

Yes, I do.

Do you like cookies?

Yes, I do.

e-learning

C. Listen and point. Make sentences.

Do you like ________?

1

candies

2

chocolate

3

cookies

4

doughnuts

D. Listen, point, and say.

A: Do you like ________?
B: Yes, I do.

Lesson 15 Drinks

Talk 1

A. Look, listen, and repeat.

I like candies.
I like chocolate.

Me, too.

I like candies. I like chocolate.

Me, too.

B. Listen, circle, and say.

1 a

b

2 a

b

Talk 2

A. Listen and sing.

Do You Want Some Milk?

I like candies. I like chocolate.
Me, too. Me, too.
Do you want some milk? Milk, milk?
No, thank you. No, thank you.

I like candies. I like chocolate.
Me, too. Me, too.
Do you want some orange juice?
Orange juice, orange juice?
No, thank you. No, thank you.

B. Look, listen, and repeat. 

Do you want some milk?

No, thank you.

Say and Act

Do you want some milk?

No, thank you.

e-learning

C. Listen and point. Make sentences.

Do you want some ________?

1

hot chocolate

2

milk

3

orange juice

4

yogurt

D. Listen, point, and say.

A: Do you want some ________?
B: No, thank you.

Alphabet Phonics Qq~Uu

Phonics Time

A. Look, listen, and repeat.

A	B	C	D	E	F	G	H	I	J	K	L	M	N	O	P	Q	R	S	T	U	V	W	X	Y	Z
a	b	c	d	e	f	g	h	i	j	k	l	m	n	o	p	q	r	s	t	u	v	w	x	y	z

e-learning

B. Listen and chant.

Q	says q, q, q	q, q, queen	q, q, quilt		
R	says r, r, r	r, r, rabbit	r, r, ring		
S	says s, s, s	s, s, seal	s, s, swan		
T	says t, t, t	t, t, tiger	t, t, top		
U	says u, u, u	u, u, umbrella	u, u, uncle		

C. Find and circle. Read along.

The queen is on a quilt.
The rabbit has a ring.
The seal plays with the swan.
The tiger plays with a top.
My uncle has an umbrella.

Fun Time
Start
1 A: Are you hungry?
B: ____________
2 I like doughnuts.
9 Do you want some yogurt?
8 Me, too.
Finish
10 Next time!
11 I like candies.
I like chocolate.
12 Let's sing on page 63.
13 No, thank you.

Go 1.
Go 2.
Go 3.
3 Next time!
4
A: Do you want some milk?
B: No, ________.
5 A: Do you like cookies?
B: Yes, I do.
6 Let's sing on page 59.
7
A: Do you like ________?
B: Yes, I do.
18 A: Are you hungry?
B: ___________
17 hot chocolate
14 A: Do you like ___________?
B: Yes, I do.
15 Return to Start!
orange juice
16
A: _______________?
B: No, thank you.

Lesson 17 Numbers

Talk 1

A. Look, listen, and repeat.

This is my brother, Bob.

Hi. Good to meet you.

This is my brother, Bob.

Hi. Good to meet you.

B. Listen, match, and say.

1

This is my brother, Tom.

2

Talk 2

A. Listen and sing.

Let's Count!

This is my brother, Joe.
Hi. Good to meet you.

Let's count, one! Let's count, two!
Let's count, three! Let's count, four!
Let's count, five!

This is my brother, Tommy.
Hi. Nice to meet you.

Let's count, one!
Let's count, two!
Let's count, three!
Let's count, four!
Let's count, five!

One! Two! Three! Four! Five!
Yeah!

1 2 3 4 5

B. Look, listen, and repeat. 

Let's count.

One, two, three, four, five!

Let's count.

One, two, three, four, five!

C. Listen and say.

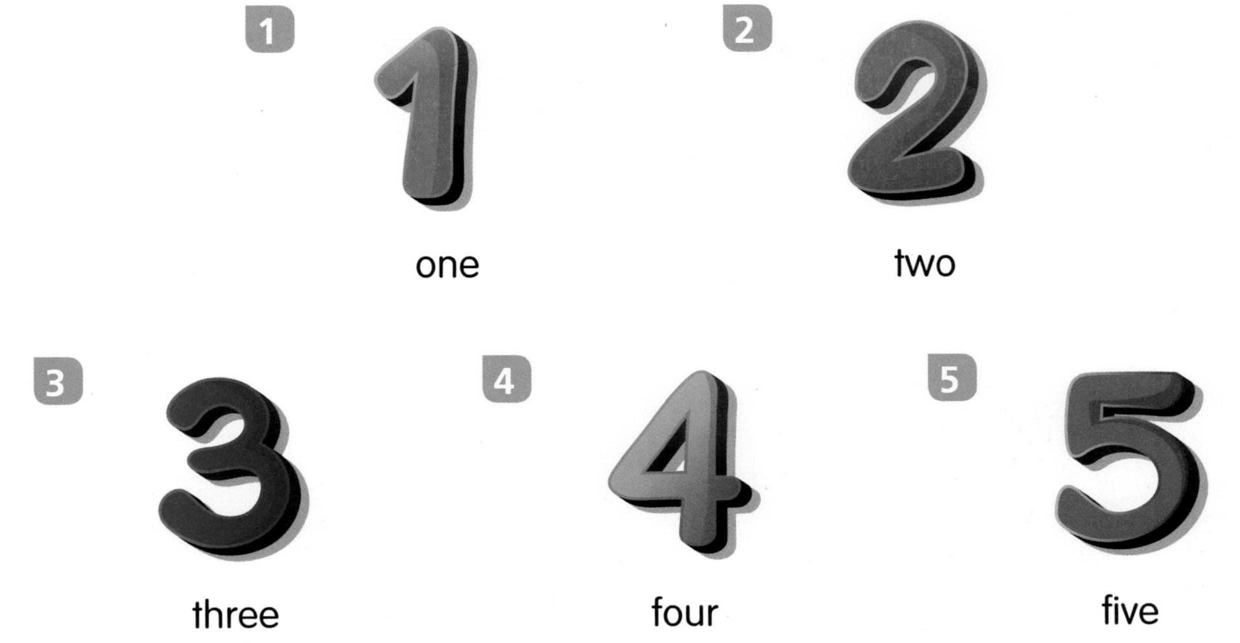

1 one

2 two

3 three

4 four

5 five

A: Let's count.
B: ________

D. Listen, point, and say.

1

2

3

4

5

A. Look, listen, and repeat.

Goodbye.

See you later.

Goodbye.

See you later.

B. Listen, circle, and say.

1 a

b

2 a

b

Talk 2

A. Listen and sing.

How Many Birds?

How many birds?
One, two, three!
Three birds.

Goodbye! Goodbye!
See you later.

How many cats?
One, two, three!
Three cats.

Goodbye! Goodbye!
See you later.

B. Look, listen, and repeat. 

How many birds?

Three.

How many birds?

Three.

e-learning

C. Listen and point. Make sentences.

How many ________?

1

birds

2

cats

3

dogs

4

rabbits

D. Listen, point, and say.

A: How many ________?
B: Three.

Alphabet Phonics Vv~Zz

Phonics Time

A. Look, listen, and repeat.

A	B	C	D	E	F	G	H	I	J	K	L	M	N	O	P	Q	R	S	T	U	V	W	X	Y	Z
a	b	c	d	e	f	g	h	i	j	k	l	m	n	o	p	q	r	s	t	u	v	w	x	y	z

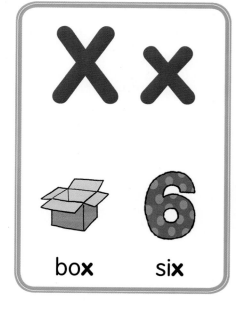

B. Listen and chant.

V	says v, v, v	v, v, vet	v, v, violin  
W	says w, w, w	w, w, water	w, w, wolf  
X	says x, x, x	x, x, box	x, x, six  
Y	says y, y, y	y, y, yak	y, y, yogurt  
Z	says z, z, z	z, z, zebra	z, z, zoo  

C. Find and circle. Read along.

The vet plays the violin.
The wolf drinks water.
The ox has six boxes.
The yak likes the yogurt.
The zebra is in the zoo.

ZOO

Fun Time
4
A: Let's count.
B: One,___,____,____,five.
4
5 two four
3 A: How many birds?
B: ______
6 Next time!
1
2 one
7
A: This is my brother, Joe.
B: Hi. ____________
1 This is my brother.
8 Return to Start!
Start

Go 1. Go 2. Go 3.
Finish
18 See you later.
No, thank you.
17 Goodbye.
16
A: How many ____?
B: ______
15 Next time!
14 four five
13 Let's sing on page 75.
12 Good to meet you.
11 Three dogs
10 Let's sing on page 71.
9
A: ______________?
B: Three.

Lesson 20

Assessment Test 2

Listening

A. Listen and check.

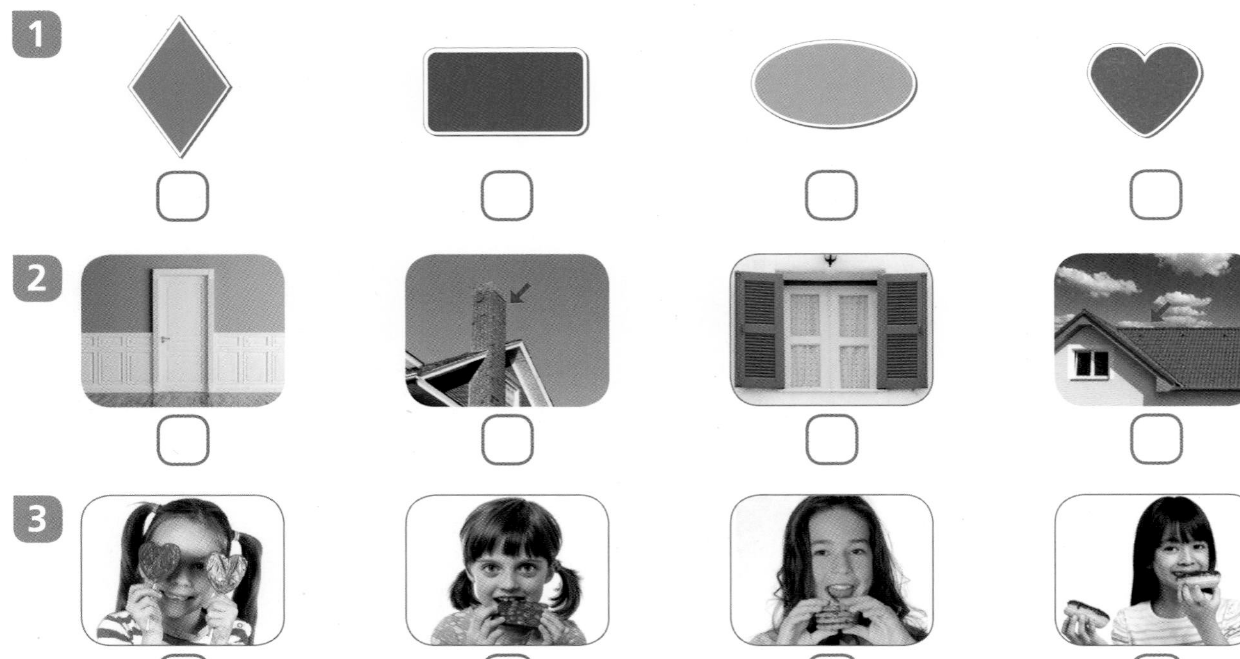

B. Listen and choose O or X.

C. Listen and circle.

D. Listen and number.

Reading Read and check.

- ◯ It's a heart.
- ◯ It's a rectangle.

- ◯ It's red. Stop!
- ◯ It's yellow. Stop!

- ◯ This is my brother.
- ◯ See you later.

- ◯ Is it a chimney?
- ◯ How many doors?

- ◯ I like candies.
- ◯ I like chocolate.

- ◯ Here you are.
- ◯ No, thank you.

Writing Match and trace.

1 

• • I like candies.

2 
• • Thank you.

3 
• • How many cookies?

4 
• • Goodbye.

Speaking

e-learning

A. Listen, point, and answer.

B. Listen and answer.

1

2

3

4

Syllabus

Lesson	Topic	Language	Key Vocabulary
Lesson 1	First Day at School	What's your name? - I'm Amy. Hello, everyone. I'm Rina Johns. - Hello, Ms. Johns.	Mark Jenny Tylor Amy
Lesson 2	Greetings	How are you today? - Good. Nice to meet you. - Nice to meet you, too.	good not so good great bad
Lesson 3	Step Up 1	Alphabet Phonics Aa~Dd Lessons 1~2 Review	Phonics: ant, apple, ball, bear, cake, cat, dog, doll
Lesson 4	Classroom	What's this? - It's a blackboard. Is this a pencil case? - Yes, it is. / No, it isn't.	blackboard computer desk television
Lesson 5	Toys	What's that? - It's a yo-yo. Let's play. - Okay.	ball bat jump rope yo-yo
Lesson 6	Step Up 2	Alphabet Phonics Ee~Hh Lessons 4~5 Review	Phonics: egg, elephant, farm, fox, goat, goose, horse, house
Lesson 7	Colors	What color is it? - It's green. Sit down, please. - Sure.	blue green red yellow
Lesson 8	Shapes	Draw a star. - Okay. Oops, I'm sorry. - That's okay.	circle square star triangle
Lesson 9	Step Up 3	Alphabet Phonics Ii~Ll Lessons 7~8 Review	Phonics: iguana, Indian, jacket, jet, king, kite, lemon, lion
Lesson 10	**Assessment Test 1** Lessons 1~9 Review		

Lesson	Topic	Language	Key Vocabulary
Lesson 11	More Shapes	What shape is it? - It's a rectangle. What color is the traffic light? - It's red. Stop!	diamond heart oval rectangle
Lesson 12	House	Is it a door? - Yes, it is. Here you are. - Thank you.	chimney door roof window
Lesson 13	Step Up 4	Alphabet Phonics Mm~Pp Lessons 11~12 Review	Phonics: man, milk, nurse, nuts, octopus, ox, pig, pizza
Lesson 14	Snacks	Do you like cookies? - Yes, I do. Are you hungry? - Yes, I am. / No, I'm not.	candies chocolate cookies doughnuts
Lesson 15	Drinks	Do you want some milk? - No, thank you. I like candies. I like chocolate. - Me, too.	hot chocolate milk orange juice yogurt
Lesson 16	Step Up 5	Alphabet Phonics Qq~Uu Lessons 14~15 Review	Phonics: queen, quilt, rabbit, ring, seal, swan, tiger, top, umbrella, uncle
Lesson 17	Numbers	Let's count. - One, two, three, four, five! This is my brother, Bob. - Hi. Good to meet you.	one two three four five
Lesson 18	Counting	How many birds? - Three. Goodbye. - See you later.	birds cats dogs rabbits
Lesson 19	Step Up 6	Alphabet Phonics Vv~Zz Lessons 17~18 Review	Phonics: vet, violin, water, wolf, box, six, yak, yogurt, zebra, zoo
Lesson 20	**Assessment Test 2** Lessons 11~19 Review		

Flashcard List

Mark	Jenny	Tylor
Amy	good	not so good
great	bad	blackboard
computer	desk	television
ball	bat	jump rope
yo-yo	blue	green
red	yellow	circle
square	star	triangle
diamond	heart	oval
rectangle	chimney	door
roof	window	candies
chocolate	cookies	doughnuts
hot chocolate	milk	orange juice
yogurt	one	two
three	four	five
birds	cats	dogs
rabbits		

Lesson 1 First Day at School

	Vocabulary	Meaning	Sentence
1	everyone	모두, 여러분	Hello, everyone.
2	hello	안녕하세요	Hello, everyone.
3	hi	안녕	Hi, Tommy!
4	I	나는, 내가	I'm Rina Johns.
5	Ms.	~ 씨	Hello, Ms. Johns.
6	name	이름	What's your name?
7	what	무엇	What's your name?
8	your	너의	What's your name?

Lesson 2 Greetings

	Vocabulary	Meaning	Sentence
1	bad	나쁜	Bad.
2	good	(기분) 좋은	Good.
3	great	정말 좋은	Great.
4	how	어떻게	How are you today?
5	meet	만나다	Nice to meet you.
6	nice	좋은	Nice to meet you.
7	not so good	별로예요	Not so good.
8	today	오늘	How are you today?
9	too	~도 역시	Nice to meet you, too.
10	you	너	Nice to meet you.

Lesson 5 Toys

	Vocabulary	Meaning	Sentence
1	ball	공	It's a ball.
2	bat	야구 방망이	It's a bat.
3	jump rope	줄넘기	It's a jump rope.
4	it	그것	It's a yo-yo.
5	okay	네, 좋아요	Okay.
6	pencil	연필	Is this a pencil?
7	play	놀다	Let's play.
8	that	저것	What's that?
9	yes	응, 네	Yes, it is.
10	yo-yo	요요	It's a yo-yo.

Lesson 6 Alphabet Phonics Ee~Hh

	Vocabulary	Meaning	Sentence
1	egg	달걀	The elephant has an egg.
2	elephant	코끼리	The elephant has an egg.
3	farm	농장	The fox plays on the farm.
4	fox	여우	The fox plays on the farm.
5	goat	염소	The goose plays with the goat.
6	goose	거위	The goose plays with the goat.
7	horse	말	The horse is in the house.
8	house	집	The horse is in the house.
9	in	~안에	The horse is in the house.
10	on	~(위)에	The fox plays on the farm.

Lesson 3 Alphabet Phonics Aa~Dd

	Vocabulary	Meaning	Sentence
1	ant	개미	The ant likes the apple.
2	apple	사과	The ant likes the apple.
3	ball	공	The bear likes the ball.
4	bear	곰	The bear likes the ball.
5	cake	케이크	The cat likes the cake.
6	cat	고양이	The cat likes the cake.
7	dog	개	The dog likes the doll.
8	doll	인형	The dog likes the doll.
9	go	가다	Go 1.
10	like	좋아하다	The dog likes the doll.

Lesson 4 Classroom

	Vocabulary	Meaning	Sentence
1	blackboard	칠판	It's a blackboard.
2	computer	컴퓨터	It's a computer.
3	desk	책상	It's a desk.
4	it	그것	It's a blackboard.
5	no	아니요	No, it isn't.
6	pencil case	필통	Is this a pencil case?
7	television	텔레비전	It's a television.
8	this	이것	What's this?
9	what	무엇	What's this?
10	yes	응, 네	Yes, it is.

Lesson 7 Colors

	Vocabulary	Meaning	Sentence
1	blue	파란	It's blue.
2	color	색깔	What color is it?
3	down	아래에	Sit down, please.
4	green	초록의	It's green.
5	play	놀다	Let's play.
6	please	제발 (부탁할 때 공손히 덧붙이는 말)	Sit down, please.
7	red	빨간	It's red.
8	sit	앉다	Sit down, please.
9	sure	네, 물론이죠	Sure.
10	yellow	노란	It's yellow.

Lesson 8 Shapes

	Vocabulary	Meaning	Sentence
1	circle	동그라미	Draw a circle.
2	draw	그리다	Draw a star.
3	okay	괜찮은	That's okay.
4	oops	이런	Oops, I'm sorry.
5	sit	앉다	Sit down, please.
6	sorry	미안한	Oops, I'm sorry.
7	square	정사각형	Draw a square.
8	star	별 (모양)	Draw a star.
9	that	저것, 그것	That's okay.
10	triangle	삼각형	Draw a triangle.

Lesson 9 Alphabet Phonics [i~L]

	Vocabulary	Meaning	Sentence
1	fly	날리다	The king flies a kite.
2	iguana	이구아나	The Indian plays with the iguana.
3	Indian	인디언	The Indian plays with the iguana.
4	jacket	재킷	The jacket is on the jet.
5	jet	제트기	The jacket is on the jet.
6	king	왕	The king flies a kite.
7	kite	연	The king flies a kite.
8	lemon	레몬	The lion licks a lemon.
9	lick	핥다	The lion licks a lemon.
10	lion	사자	The lion licks a lemon.

Lesson 11 More Shapes

	Vocabulary	Meaning	Sentence
1	color	색깔	What color is the traffic light?
2	diamond	마름모꼴	It's a diamond.
3	green	초록의	It's green.
4	heart	하트 (모양)	It's a heart.
5	oval	타원형	It's an oval.
6	rectangle	직사각형	It's a rectangle.
7	red	빨간	It's red. Stop!
8	shape	모양	What shape is it?
9	stop	멈추다	It's red. Stop!
10	traffic light	신호등	What color is the traffic light?

Lesson 14 Snacks

	Vocabulary	Meaning	Sentence
1	candy	사탕	Do you like candies?
2	chocolate	초콜릿	Do you like chocolate?
3	cookie	쿠키	Do you like cookies?
4	doughnut	도넛	Do you like doughnuts?
5	hungry	배가 고픈	Are you hungry?
6	I	나는, 내가	Yes, I am.
7	like	좋아하다	Do you like cookies?
8	not	~아니다	No, I'm not.
9	yes	네, 응	Yes, I am.
10	you	당신, 너	Are you hungry?

Lesson 15 Drinks

	Vocabulary	Meaning	Sentence
1	candy	사탕	I like candies.
2	hot chocolate	코코아	Do you want some hot chocolate?
3	like	좋아하다	I like candies.
4	Me, too.	나도 그래요.	Me, too.
5	milk	우유	Do you want some milk?
6	No, thank you.	괜찮아요.	No, thank you.
7	orange juice	오렌지 주스	Do you want some orange juice?
8	some	조금, 약간의	Do you want some milk?
9	want	원하다	Do you want some milk?
10	yogurt	요구르트	Do you want some yogurt?

Lesson 12 House

	Vocabulary	Meaning	Sentence
1	chimney	굴뚝	Is it a chimney?
2	door	문	Is it a door?
3	draw	그리다	Draw a star.
4	here	여기에	Here you are.
5	it	그것	Is it a door?
6	roof	지붕	Is it a roof?
7	star	별 (모양)	Draw a star.
8	thank	감사하다	Thank you.
9	window	창문	Is it a window?
10	you	당신, 너	Here you are.

Lesson 13 Alphabet Phonics Mm~Pp

	Vocabulary	Meaning	Sentence
1	drink	마시다	The man drinks milk.
2	eat	먹다	The nurse eats nuts.
3	man	남자, 사람	The man drinks milk.
4	milk	우유	The man drinks milk.
5	nurse	간호사	The nurse eats nuts.
6	nuts	견과류	The nurse eats nuts.
7	octopus	문어	The ox likes the octopus.
8	ox	황소	The ox likes the octopus.
9	pig	돼지	The pig likes pizza.
10	pizza	피자	The pig likes pizza.

Lesson 16 Alphabet Phonics Qq~Uu

	Vocabulary	Meaning	Sentence
1	queen	여왕	The queen is on a quilt.
2	quilt	퀼트	The queen is on a quilt.
3	rabbit	토끼	The rabbit has a ring.
4	ring	반지	The rabbit has a ring.
5	seal	바다표범	The seal plays with the swan.
6	swan	백조	The seal plays with the swan.
7	tiger	호랑이	The tiger plays with a top.
8	top	팽이	The tiger plays with a top.
9	umbrella	우산	My uncle has an umbrella.
10	uncle	삼촌	My uncle has an umbrella.

Lesson 17 Numbers

	Vocabulary	Meaning	Sentence
1	brother	형제	This is my brother.
2	count	수를 세다	Let's count.
3	meet	만나다	Good to meet you.
4	my	나의	This is my brother, Bob.
5	this	이 사람, 이것	This is my brother, Bob.
6	one	하나, 1	One, two, three, four, five!
7	two	둘, 2	One, two, three, four, five!
8	three	셋, 3	One, two, three, four, five!
9	four	넷, 4	One, two, three, four, five!
10	five	다섯, 5	One, two, three, four, five!

Lesson 18 Counting

	Vocabulary	Meaning	Sentence
1	bird	새	How many birds?
2	cat	고양이	How many cats?
3	dog	개	How many dogs?
4	goodbye	잘 가요	Goodbye.
5	how	얼마나	How many birds?
6	later	나중에	See you later.
7	many	많은	How many birds?
8	rabbit	토끼	How many rabbits?
9	see	보다	See you later.
10	three	셋, 3	Three birds.

Lesson 19 Alphabet Phonics Vv~Zz

	Vocabulary	Meaning	Sentence
1	box	상자	The ox has six boxes.
2	six	여섯, 6	The ox has six boxes.
3	vet	수의사	The vet plays the violin.
4	violin	바이올린	The vet plays the violin.
5	water	물	The wolf drinks water.
6	wolf	늑대	The wolf drinks water.
7	yak	야크	The yak likes the yogurt.
8	yogurt	요구르트	The yak likes the yogurt.
9	zebra	얼룩말	The zebra is in the zoo.
10	zoo	동물원	The zebra is in the zoo.

Answers

Student Book Answers

Lesson 1 First Day at School

B. Listen, match, and say. p. 7

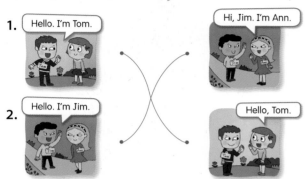

Lesson 2 Greetings

B. Listen, check, and say. p. 11

1. ⓐ 2. ⓑ

Lesson 3 Alphabet Phonics Aa~Dd

C. Find and circle. Read along. p. 15

Fun Time pp. 16~17

1. Hello, Tom.
4. Tim
5.
7. Great. / Good.
8. Hello.
9. I'm Mark.
13. Nice to meet you, too.
14. Not so good.
15. What's your name

Lesson 4 Classroom

B. Listen, circle, and say. p. 19

1. ⓐ 2. ⓑ

Lesson 5 Toys

B. Listen, match, and say. p. 23

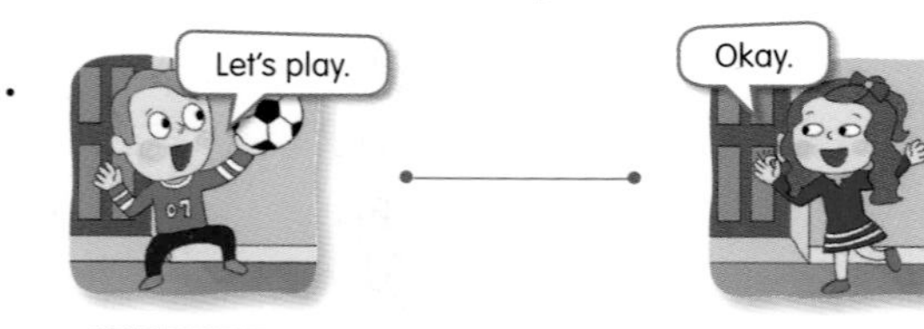

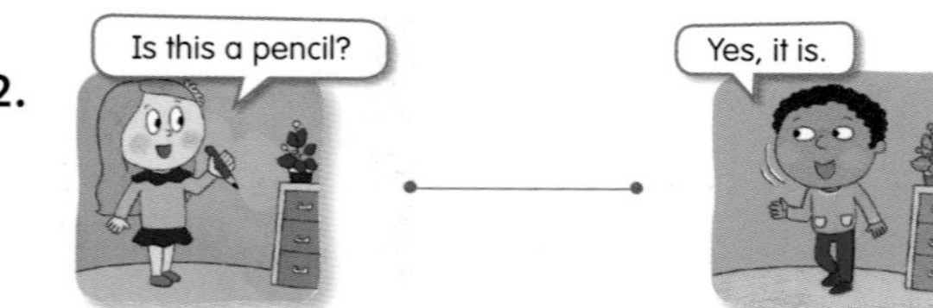

Lesson 6 Alphabet Phonics Ee~Hh

C. Find and circle. Read along. p. 27

Fun Time pp. 28~29

1. It's a television.
5. It's a desk.
6. What's this?
7. What's that
8. Yes, it is.
12. blackboard
15.
16. jump rope

Lesson 7 Colors

B. Listen, check, and say. p. 31

1. ⓑ 2. ⓑ

Lesson 8 Shapes

B. Listen, circle, and say. p. 35

1. ⓐ 2. ⓑ

Lesson 9 Alphabet Phonics Ii~Ll

C. Find and circle. Read along. p. 39

Fun Time pp. 40~41

1. It's red.
3. green
4. That's okay.
5. (circle)
7. What color is it
9. It's blue.
13. star
14. Sure.
15. Okay.

Lesson 10 Assessment Test 1

Listening pp. 42~43

A. 1.  2.  3. 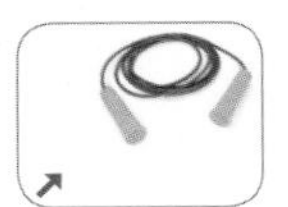

B. 1. × 2. × 3. ○ 4. ○ 5. × 6. ○

C. 1.  2.  3. 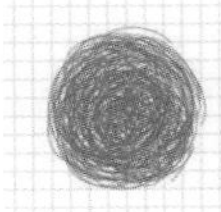

4.  5.  6. 

D. 1. ⓓ 2. ⓒ 3. ⓐ 4. ⓑ

Reading p. 44

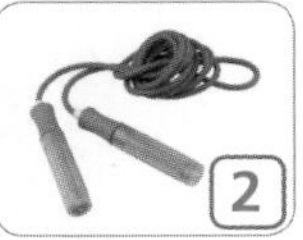

Ken 5 | 6 | 1

4 | 3 | 2

Writing p. 44

1. 
2. 
3. 
4.

Draw a kite.

It's a computer.

What's your name?

How are you today?

Speaking p. 45

A. 1. It's a blackboard.
2. Good.
3. Okay.
4. It's a yo-yo.

B. 1. It's an elephant.
2. I'm Ann.
3. No, it isn't.
4. Great.

Lesson 11 More Shapes

B. Listen, number, and say. p. 47

 3

 2

 1

Lesson 12 House

B. Listen, match, and say. p. 51

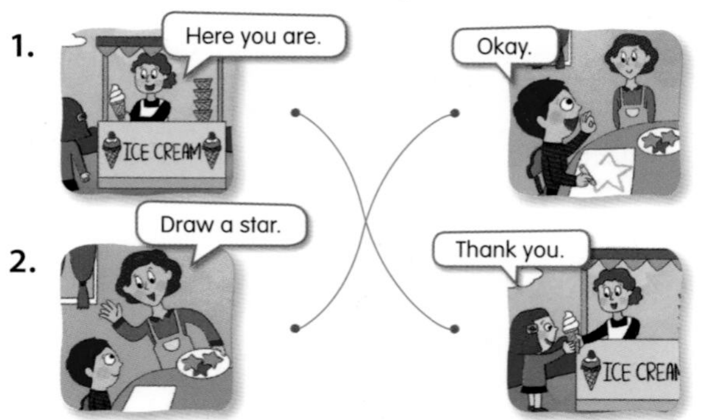

Lesson 13 Alphabet Phonics Mm~Pp

C. Find and circle. Read along. p. 55

Fun Time pp. 56~57

1. It's red.
5. Thank you.
7. Yes, it is.
8.
9. Here you are.
10. It's a diamond.
12. It's an oval.
14. heart
16. What shape is it?
17. Is it a roof

Lesson 14 Snacks

B. Listen, check, and say. p. 59

1. ⓐ 2. ⓑ

Lesson 15 Drinks

B. Listen, circle, and say. p. 63

1. ⓑ 2. ⓐ

Lesson 16 Alphabet Phonics Qq~Uu

B. Find and circle. Read along. p. 67

Fun Time pp. 68~69

1. Yes, I am.
4. thank you
5.
7. candies
8. Me, too.
9. 
13. No, thank you.
14. chocolate
16. Do you want some orange juice
17. hot chocolate
18. No, I'm not.

Lesson 17 Numbers

B. Listen, match, and say. p. 71

Lesson 18 Counting

B. Listen, circle, and say. p. 75

1. ⓑ 2. ⓑ

Lesson 19 Alphabet Phonics Vv~Zz

B. Find and circle. Read along. p. 79

Fun Time pp. 80~81

2. one
3. Three.
4. two, three, four
5. four
7. Good to meet you.
9. How many rabbits
11. 
12. Good to meet you.
14. five
16. cats, Two.
17. Goodbye.
18. See you later.

Lesson 20 Assessment Test 2

Listening pp. 82~83

A. 1.  2.  3. 

B. 1. ○ 2. ○ 3. × 4. ○ 5. ○ 6. ×

C. 1.  2. 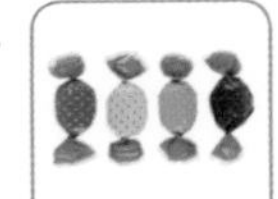 3. 

4.  5.  6. 

D.

 2

 4

 1

 3

Reading p. 84

1. It's a heart.
2. It's red. Stop!
3. See you later.
4. Is it a chimney?
5. I like chocolate.
6. Here you are.

Writing p. 84

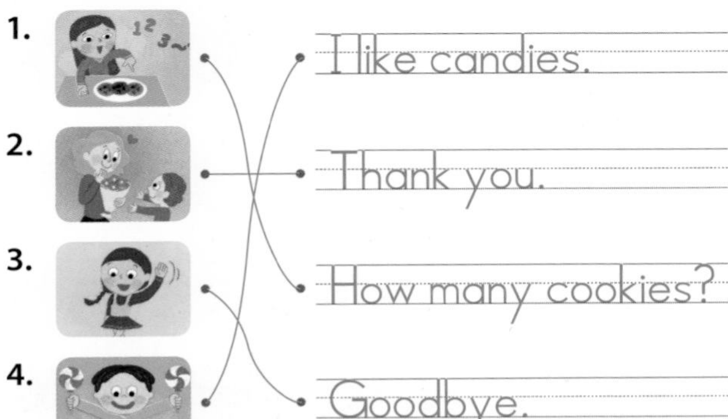

1.
2.
3.
4.
I like candies.
Thank you.
How many cookies?
Goodbye.

Speaking p. 85

A. 1. Thank you.
2. Three.
3. Yes, I am.
4. No, thank you.

B. 1. It's red.
2. It's a rectangle.
3. No, thank you.
4. Four.

Workbook Answers

Lesson 1 First Day at School pp. 4~5

A. 1. ⓐ Hello, everyone. I'm Rina Johns.
ⓑ Hello, Ms. Johns.

2. ⓐ I'm Amy.
ⓑ What's your name?

B. 2. ⓐ

C. 1. I'm Mark.
2. I'm Amy. I'm Amy.
3. I'm Tylor. I'm Tylor.
4. I'm Jenny. I'm Jenny.

Lesson 2 Greetings pp. 6~7

A. 1. ⓐ Nice to meet you.
ⓑ Nice to meet you, too.

2. ⓐ How are you today?
ⓑ Good.

B. 2. ⓑ

C.

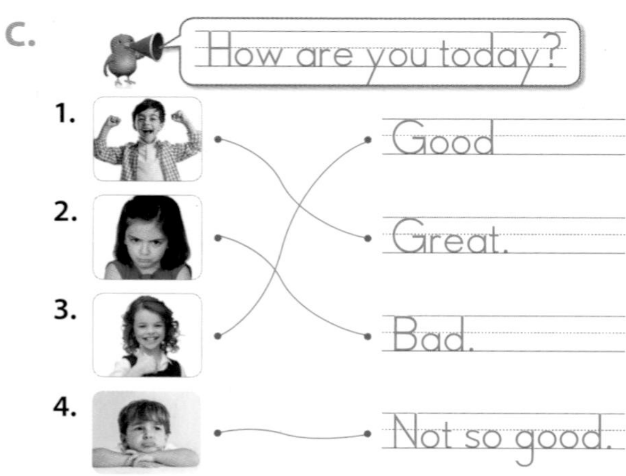

Lesson 3 Alphabet Phonics Aa~Dd

pp. 8~9

A.

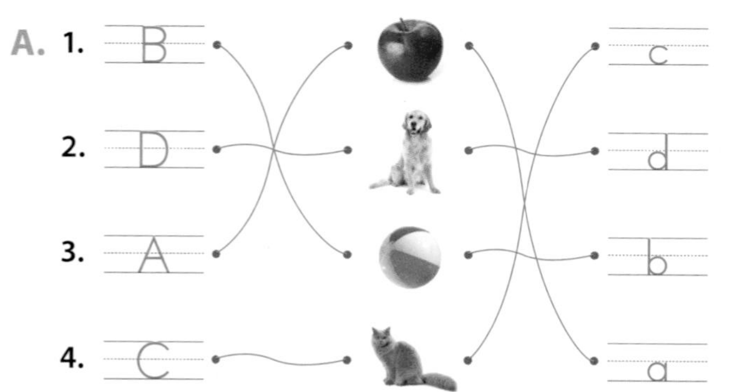

B. 1. ant
2. bear
3. cake
4. doll

C. 1. 

2. 

3. 

4. 

D. 1.  Hello. I'm Annie.

2. Bad.

3. Great.

4.  Nice to meet you.

Lesson 4 Classroom

pp. 10~11

A. 1. ⓐ Yes, it is.

ⓑ Is this a pencil case?

2. ⓐ It's a blackboard.

ⓑ What's this?

B. 1. ⓐ 2. ⓑ

C. 1. It's a desk. ○

2. It's a television. ×

3. It's a blackboard. ○

4. It's a computer. ×

Lesson 5 Toys

pp. 12~13

A. 1. ⓐ Let's play.

ⓑ Okay.

2. ⓐ What's that?

ⓑ It's a yo-yo.

B. 1. ⓐ 2. ⓑ

C. 1. It's a jump rope.

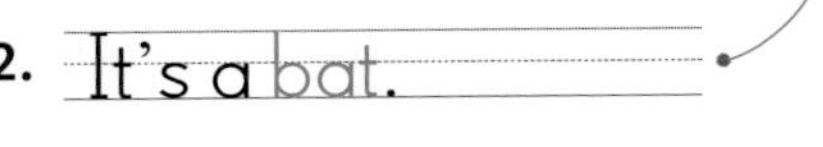

2. It's a bat.

3. It's a yo-yo.

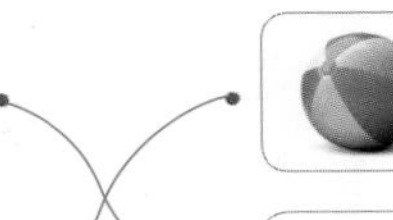

4. It's a ball.

Lesson 6 Alphabet Phonics Ee~Hh

pp. 14~15

A. 1. 2. 3. 4.

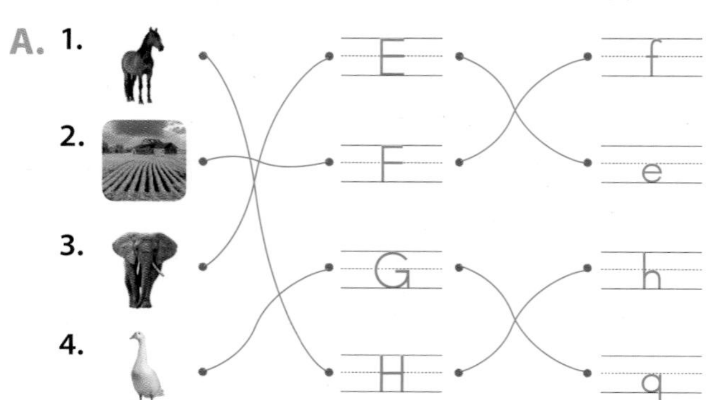

B.
1. g j d l t h g u o t (e g g)
2. b a e (g o a t) e g o o y
3. s i e (h o u s e) k e b t r
4. (f o x) e k t l r s i c e f e r

C. 1. ○ 2. × 3. ○ 4. ○

D.
1. It's a pencil case. It's a pencil case.
2. What's this? What's this?
3. It's a computer. It's a computer.
4. Let's play. Let's play.

Lesson 7 Colors

pp. 16~17

B. 1. ⓐ Sit down, please.

ⓑ Sure.

2. ⓐ It's green.

ⓑ What color is it?

B. 1. ⓐ 2. ⓐ

C. What color is it?

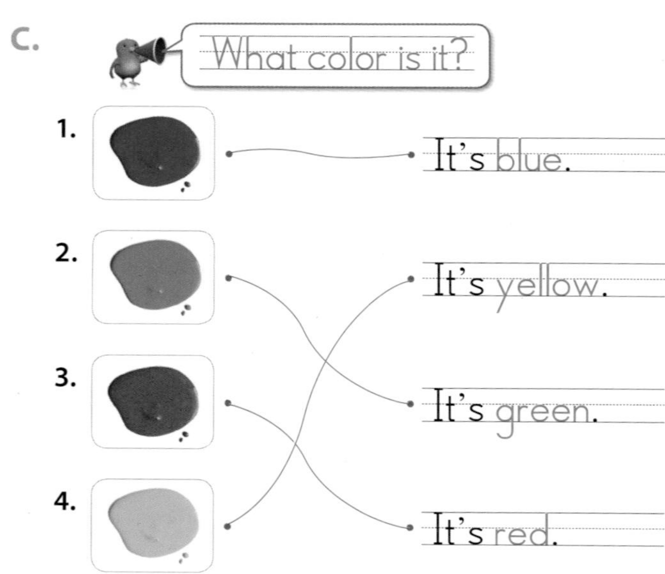

Lesson 8 Shapes

pp. 18~19

A. 1. ⓐ That's okay.

ⓑ Oops, I'm sorry.

2. ⓐ Okay.

ⓑ Draw a star.

B. 1. Oops, I'm sorry.

2. Sit down, please.

C. 1. Draw a square. 

2. Draw a star. 

3. Draw a circle. 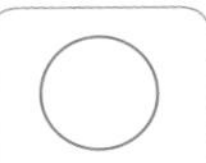

4. Draw a triangle. 

Lesson 9 Alphabet Phonics Ii~Ll pp. 20~21

A. 1. I  i

2. J  j

3. K  k

4. L  l

B. 1. I – Indian

2. J – jacket

3. K – kite

4. L – lion

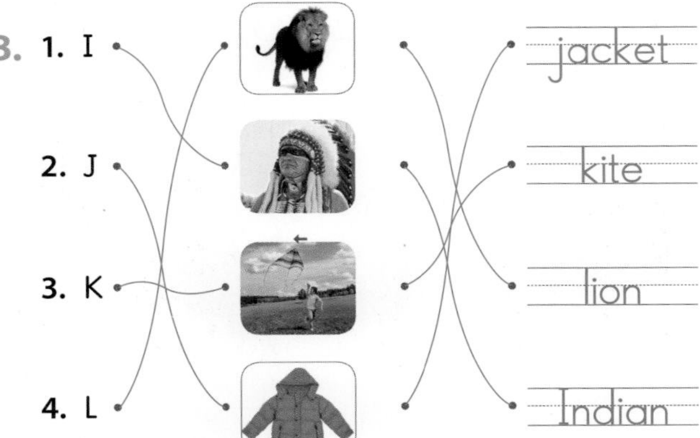

C. 1.  2. 

3.  4. 

D. 1.  – It's blue.

2. 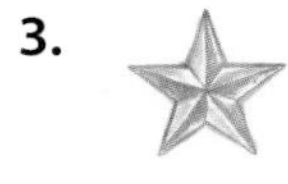 – What color is it?

3.  – Draw a star.

4.  – Sit down, please.

Lesson 11 More Shapes pp. 22~23

A. 1. ⓐ What color is the traffic light?

ⓑ It's red. Stop!

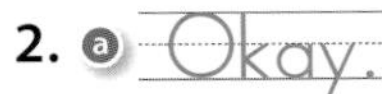
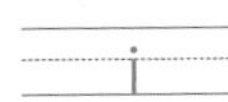

2. ⓐ What shape is it?

ⓑ It's a rectangle.

B. 1. ⓐ 2. ⓐ

C. 1. It's an oval. ×

2. It's a diamond. ○

3. It's a rectangle. ○

4. It's a heart. ×

Lesson 12 House

pp. 24~25

A. 1. ⓐ Here you are.

ⓑ Thank you.

2. ⓐ Yes, it is.

ⓑ Is it a door?

B. 1. Here you are.

2. Thank you.

C. 1. Is it a door?

2. Is it a chimney?

3. Is it a roof?

4. Is it a window?

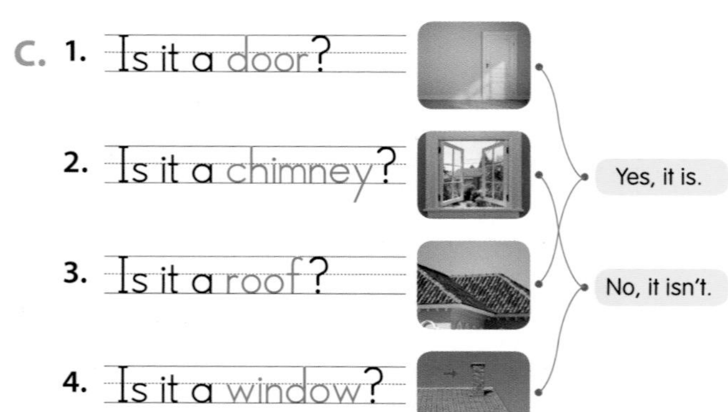

Lesson 13 Alphabet Phonics Mm~Pp

pp. 26~27

A. 1. N

2. O

3. P

4. M

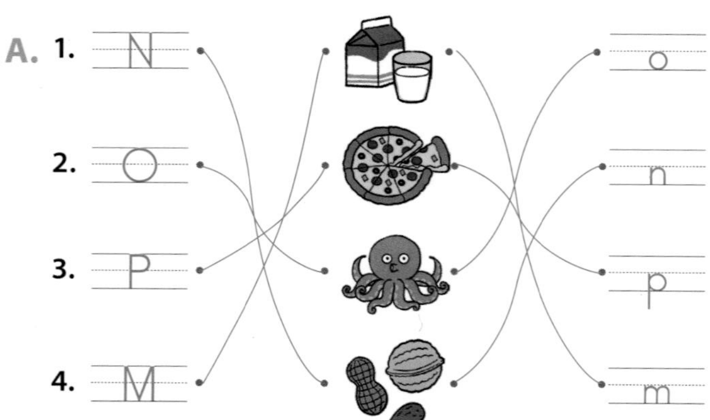

B. 1. ba(nurse)egox

2. u(pig)sekebtrh

3. manursieh(ox)

4. (man)opigmon

C. 1. ○ 2. ×

3. ○ 4. ×

D. 1. It's a heart. It's a heart.

2. Here you are. Here you are.

3. Is it a window? Is it a window?

4. What shape is it? What shape is it?

Lesson 14 Snacks

pp. 28~29

A. 1. ⓐ Yes, I am.

ⓑ Are you hungry?

2. ⓐ Do you like cookies?

ⓑ Yes, I do.

B. 1. ⓑ 2. ⓐ

C. 1. Do you like candies?

2. Do you like doughnuts?

3. Do you like chocolate?

4. Do you like cookies?

Lesson 15 Drinks

pp. 30~31

A. 1. ⓐ I like candies. I like chocolate.

ⓑ Me, too.

2. ⓐ No, thank you.

ⓑ Do you want some milk?

B. 1. ⓑ 2. ⓐ

C. 1. 2. 3. 4.

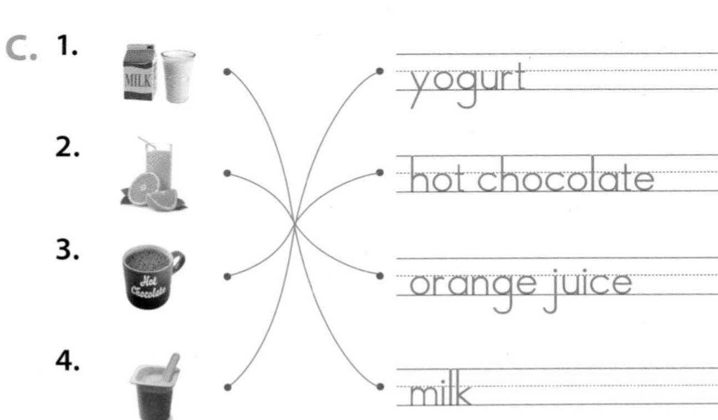

Lesson 16 Alphabet Phonics Qq~Uu

pp. 32~33

A. 1. Q q

2. R r

3. S s

4. T t

5. U u

B. 1. T

2. R

3. Q

4. U

5. S

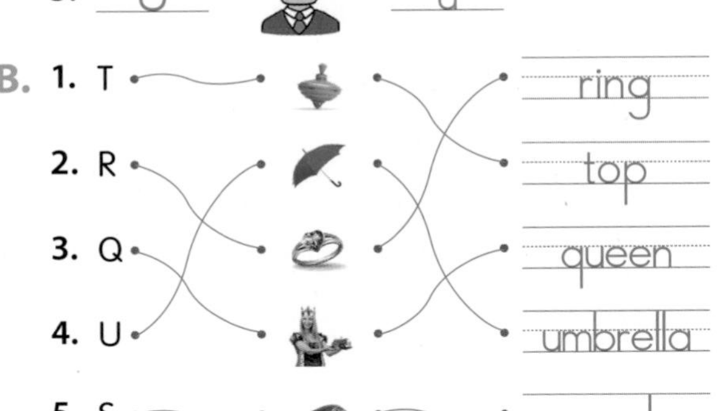

C. 1.  2. 

3.  4. 

D. 1. 
2. 
3. 
4. 

No, thank you.
I like candies.
Do you like cookies?
Do you want some yogurt?

Lesson 17 Numbers pp. 34~35

A. 1. ⓐ Hi. Good to meet you.
ⓑ This is my brother, Bob.

2. ⓐ Let's count.
ⓑ One, two, three, four, five.

B. 1. This is my brother, Tom.
2. Hi. Good to meet you.

C.  Let's count.

1. 3 ■■■□□
2. 5 ▲▲▲▲▲
3. 4 ●●●●○
4. 2 ★★☆☆☆
5. 1 ◆◇◇◇◇

One.
Two.
Three.
Four.
Five.

Lesson 18 Counting pp. 36~37

A. 1. ⓐ Goodbye.
ⓑ See you later.

2. ⓐ Three.
ⓑ How many birds?

B. 1. ○ 2. ×

C. 1. How many birds?
2. How many dogs?
3. How many rabbits?
4. How many cats?

Lesson 19 Alphabet Phonics Vv~Zz

pp. 38~39

A.

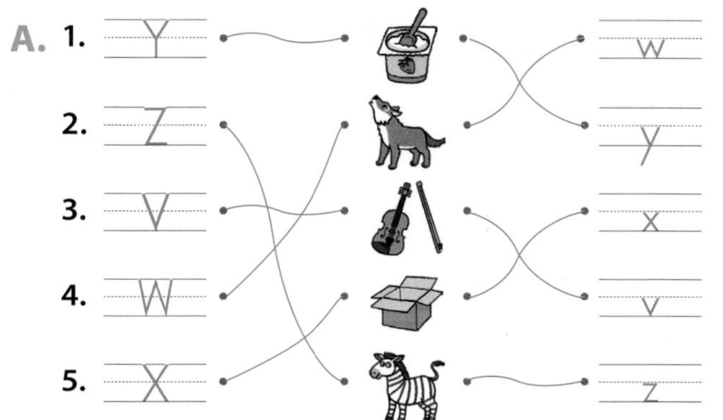

B. 1. r s e e g o x (z o o) d k t

2. m i o (v e t) y a k o r h o

3. s m a n u r (s i x) e h o x

4. m a n o o u t (y a k) m o

5. w o e d i s l t j (w a t e r)

C. 1. ○ 2. × 3. × 4. ○

D. 1. How many cats? How many cats?

2. Let's count. Let's count.

3. See you later. See you later.

4. Good to meet you. Good to meet you.

Final Test
English Town Starter Book 1

1. ③	2. ②	3. ③	4. ④	5. ④
6. ①	7. ③	8. ①	9. ②	10. ④
11. ④	12. ⑤	13. ②	14. ②	15. ⑤
16. ①	17. ③	18. ②		

19. traffic red 20. some

Memo

ENGLISH TOWN

FOR EVERYONE

STARTER

WORKBOOK

YBM

ENGLISH TOWN

FOR EVERYONE

STARTER

WORKBOOK

Contents

Lesson 1 First Day at School

A. Trace and choose.

1 ⓐ Hello, everyone. I'm Rina Johns.

ⓑ Hello, Ms. Johns.

2 ⓐ I'm Amy.

ⓑ What's your name?

B. Read and match.

1

2

ⓐ Hello, Jim.

ⓑ Hi. I'm Tom.

C. Check and trace.

1

- [ ] I'm Amy.
- [x] I'm Mark.

I'm Mark.

2

- [ ] I'm Amy.
- [ ] I'm Tylor.

I'm Amy.

3

- [ ] I'm Tylor.
- [ ] I'm Jenny.

I'm Tylor.

4

- [ ] I'm Mark.
- [ ] I'm Jenny.

I'm Jenny.

Lesson 2 Greetings

A. Trace and choose.

1 ⓐ Nice to meet you.

ⓑ Nice to meet you, too.

2 ⓐ How are you today?

ⓑ Good.

B. Read and circle.

ⓐ What's your name?

ⓑ Nice to meet you.

ⓐ Nice to meet you, too.

ⓑ I'm Kevin.

C. Match and trace.

How are you today?

1  • • Good.

2  • • Great.

3  • • Bad.

4  • • Not so good.

Lesson 3 Alphabet Phonics Aa~Dd

A. Match and trace.

1 

 c

2 

 d

3 

 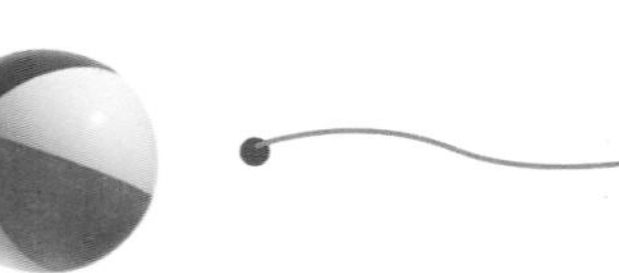  b

4 

 a

B. Circle and trace.

1 A a  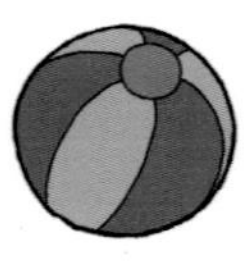 

2 B b   

3 C c   

4 D d   

C. Read and check.

1 A: What's your name?
B: I'm Mark.

☐

☐

2 A: How are you today?
B: Great.

 ☐  ☐

3 A: How are you today?
B: Not so good.

 ☐  ☐

4 A: Nice to meet you.
B: Nice to meet you, too.

 ☐  ☐

D. Match and trace.

 • • 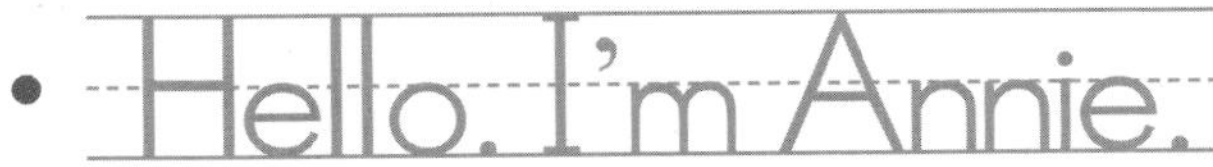

2 

• • Bad.

3  • • Great.

4  • • Nice to meet you.

Lesson 4 Classroom

A. Trace and choose.

1 a Yes, it is.

b Is this a pencil case?

2 a It's a blackboard.

b What's this?

B. Read and match.

1 

2 

ⓐ A: Is this a pencil case?
B: Yes, it is.

ⓑ A: Is this a pencil case?
B: No, it isn't.

C. Trace and choose O or X.

1 It's a desk. O X

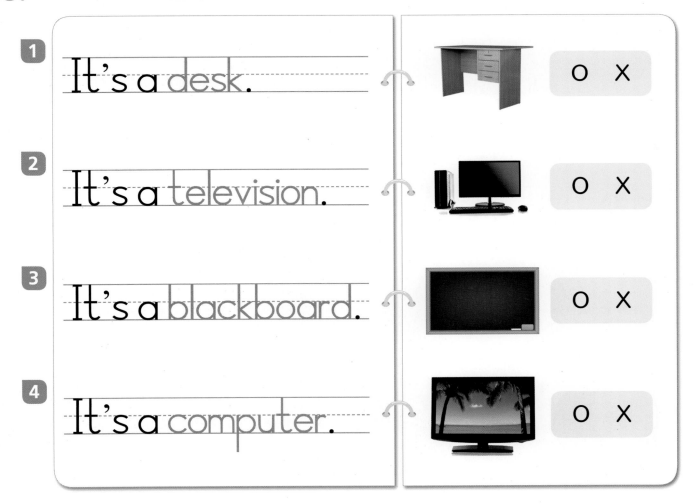

2 It's a television. O X

3 It's a blackboard. O X

4 It's a computer. O X

Lesson 5 Toys

A. Trace and choose.

1. ⓐ Let's play.

   ⓑ Okay.

2. ⓐ What's that?

   ⓑ It's a yo-yo.

B. Read and circle.

ⓐ Let's play.

ⓑ I'm sleepy.

ⓐ Is this a pencil case?

ⓑ Okay.

C. Trace and match.

1 It's a jump rope.

2 It's a bat.

3 It's a yo-yo.

4 It's a ball.

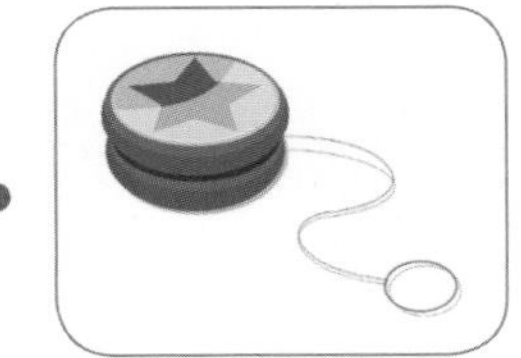

Lesson 6 Alphabet Phonics Ee~Hh

A. Match and trace.

1   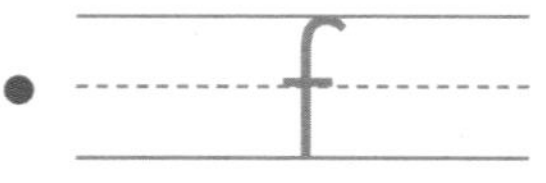

2  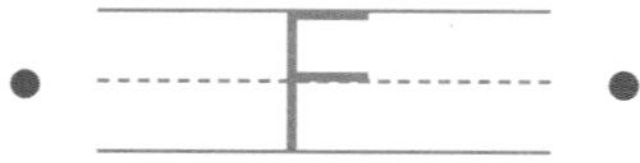 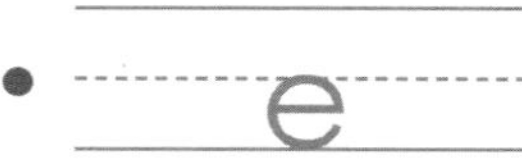

3   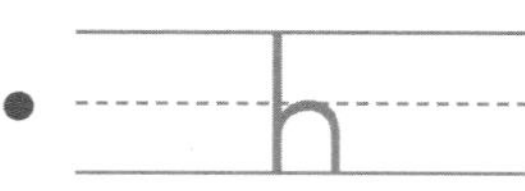

4  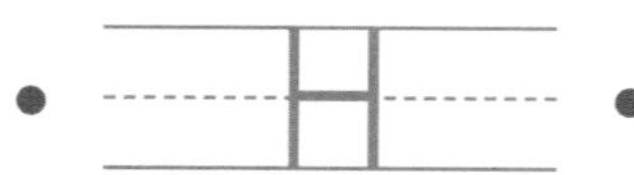 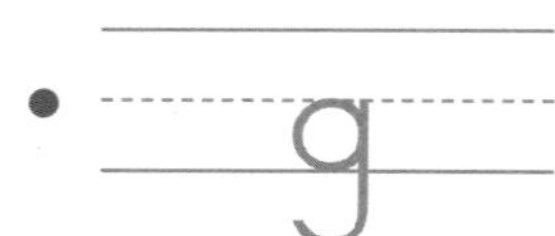

B. Find and circle.

 gjghorseter

1 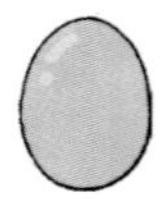 gjdlthguotegg

2  baegoategooy

3  siehousekebtr

4  foxektlrsicefer

C. Read and choose O or X.

A: What's this?
B: It's a bat.

O X

2

A: Is this a ball?
B: Yes, it is.

O X

3

A: What's that?
B: It's a yo-yo.

O X

4

A: Let's play.
B: Okay.

O X

D. Check and trace.

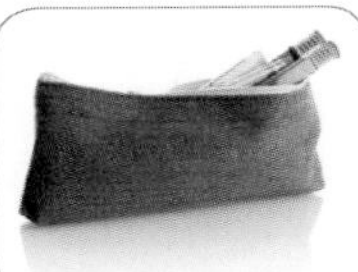

- ☐ It's a jump rope.
- ☐ It's a pencil case.

It's a pencil case.

2

- ☐ What's this?
- ☐ What's that?

What's this?

3

- ☐ It's a computer.
- ☐ It's a blackboard.

It's a computer.

4

- ☐ Let's play.
- ☐ It's a bat.

Let's play.

Lesson 7 Colors

A. Trace and choose.

1 ⓐ Sit down, please.

ⓑ Sure.

2 ⓐ It's green.

ⓑ What color is it?

B. Read and circle.

ⓐ Sit down, please.

ⓑ It's a bat.

2

ⓐ Let's play.

ⓑ Is this a pencil case?

C. Match and trace.

What color is it?

1  • It's blue.

2 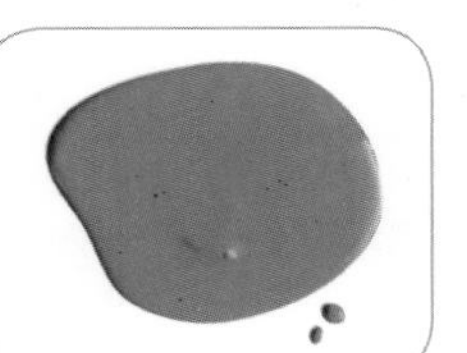 • It's yellow.

3  • It's green.

4  • It's red.

Lesson 8 Shapes

A. Trace and choose.

1 ⓐ That's okay.

ⓑ Oops, I'm sorry.

2 ⓐ Okay.

ⓑ Draw a star.

B. Read and check.

1 

- ◯ What color is it?
- ◯ Oops, I'm sorry.

2 

- ◯ That's okay.
- ◯ Sit down, please.

C. Trace and draw.

1 Draw a square. 

2 Draw a star. 

3 Draw a circle. 

4 Draw a triangle. 

Alphabet Phonics Ii~Ll

A. Circle and trace.

1 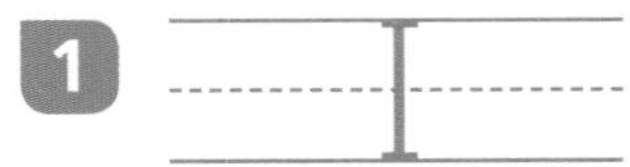   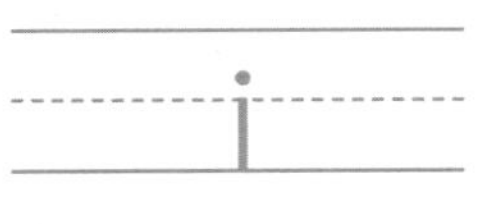

2    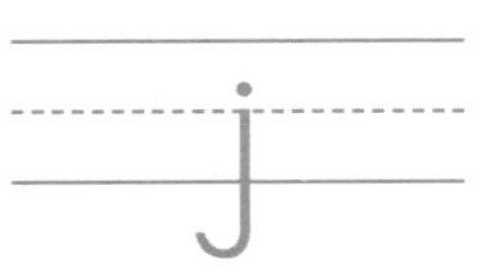

3    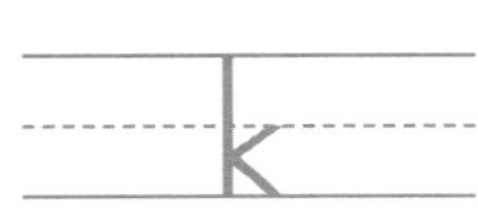

4  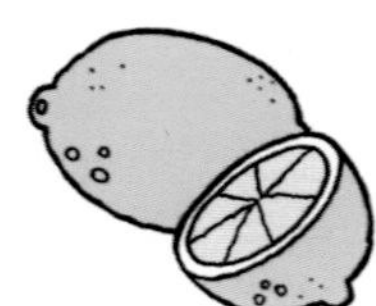 

B. Match and trace.

1 I •  • jacket

2 J • • kite

3 K • • lion

4 L • • Indian

C. Read and check.

1 A: What color is it?
B: It's yellow.

 ☐  ☐

2 A: Sit down, please.
B: Sure.

 ☐  ☐

3 A: Draw a circle.
B: Okay.

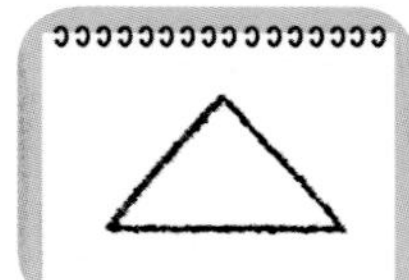 ☐ 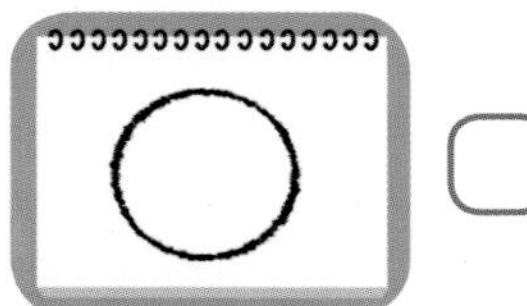 ☐

4 A: Oops! I'm sorry.
B: That's okay.

 ☐  ☐

D. Match and trace.

1  • • It's blue.

2  • • Sit down, please.

3  • • Draw a star.

4  • • What color is it?

Lesson 11 More Shapes

A. Trace and choose.

1 ⓐ What color is the traffic light?

ⓑ It's red. Stop!

2 ⓐ What shape is it?

ⓑ It's a rectangle.

B. Read and circle.

1

What color is the traffic light?

ⓐ It's red.

ⓑ It's green.

2

What color is the traffic light?

ⓐ It's green.

ⓑ It's yellow.

C. Trace and choose O or X.

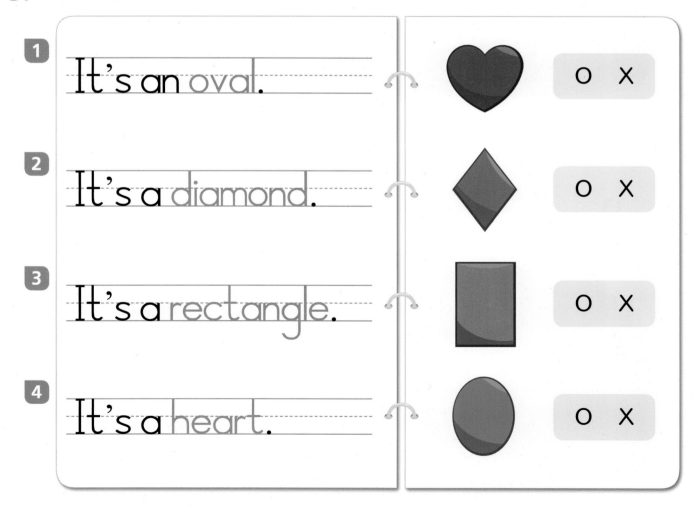

1 It's an oval. O X

2 It's a diamond. O X

3 It's a rectangle. O X

4 It's a heart. O X

Lesson 12 House

A. Trace and choose.

1 ⓐ Here you are.

ⓑ Thank you.

2 ⓐ Yes, it is.

ⓑ Is it a door?

B. Read and check.

1

- ▢ Here you are.
- ▢ It's yellow.

2

- ▢ Thank you.
- ▢ No, thank you.

C. Trace and match.

1 Is it a door?

2 Is it a chimney?

• Yes, it is.

3 Is it a roof?

• No, it isn't.

4 Is it a window?

A. Match and trace.

1 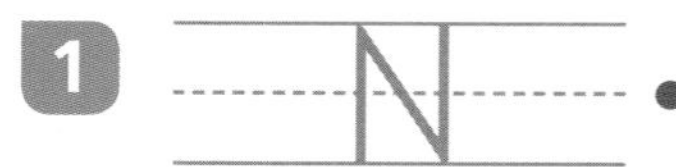

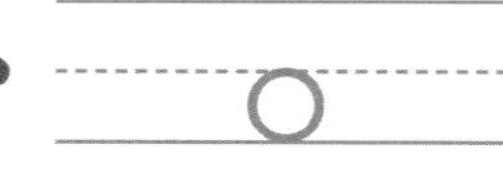

2 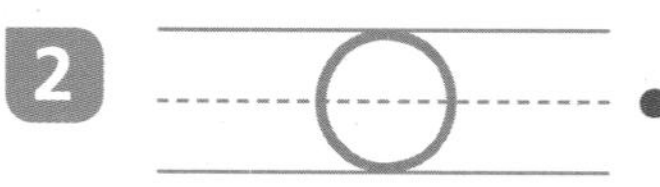

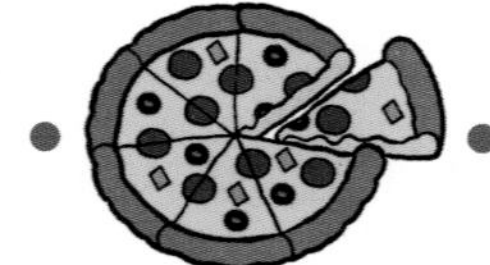
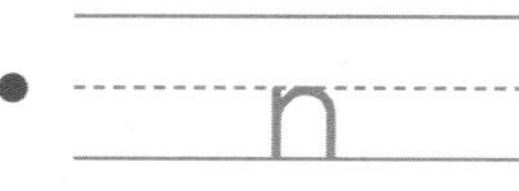

3 

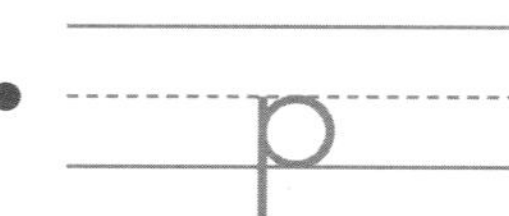

4 

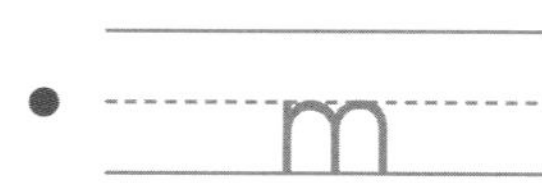

B. Find and circle.

1 

2  u p i g s e k e b t r h

3  m a n u r s i e h o x

4  m a n o p i g m o n

C. Read and choose O or X.

1 

A: Here you are.
B: Thank you.

O X

2 

A: What shape is it?
B: It's a rectangle.

O X

3 

A: Is it a chimney?
B: Yes, it is.

O X

4 

A: What color is the traffic light?
B: It's red. Stop!

O X

D. Check and trace.

1 

- ☐ It's an oval.
- ☐ It's a heart.

It's a heart.

2 

- ☐ Here you are.
- ☐ Stop!

Here you are.

3 

- ☐ Is it a roof?
- ☐ Is it a window?

Is it a window?

4 

- ☐ What shape is it?
- ☐ It's red.

What shape is it?

Lesson 14 Snacks

A. Trace and choose.

1
ⓐ Yes, I am.
ⓑ Are you hungry?

2
ⓐ Do you like cookies?
ⓑ Yes, I do.

B. Read and match.

1 

2 

ⓐ A: Are you hungry?
B: Yes, I am.

ⓑ A: Are you hungry?
B: No, I'm not.

C. Check and trace.

1 

- ☐ Do you like candies?
- ☐ Do you like cookies?

2 

- ☐ Do you like chocolate?
- ☐ Do you like doughnuts?

3 

- ☐ Do you like chocolate?
- ☐ Do you like candies?

4 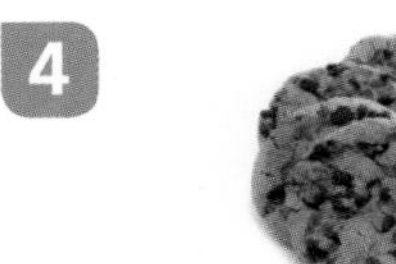

- ☐ Do you like cookies?
- ☐ Do you like doughnuts?

Lesson 15 Drinks

A. Trace and choose.

1 ⓐ I like candies. I like chocolate.

ⓑ Me, too.

2 ⓐ No, thank you.

ⓑ Do you want some milk?

B. Read and circle.

1 A: I like candies.
I like chocolate.
B: Me, too.

ⓐ 

ⓑ 

2 A: I like cookies.
I like doughnuts.
B: Me, too.

ⓐ 

ⓑ 

D. Match and trace.

Do you want some ________?

1  • • yogurt

2  • • hot chocolate

3 

• • orange juice

4  • • milk

Lesson

16 Alphabet Phonics Qq~Uu

A. Circle and trace.

1  Q   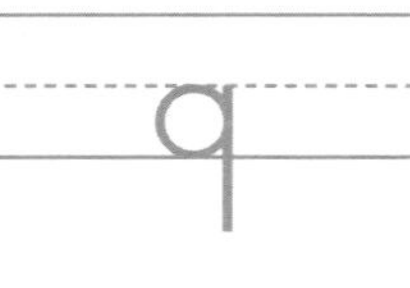 q

2  R   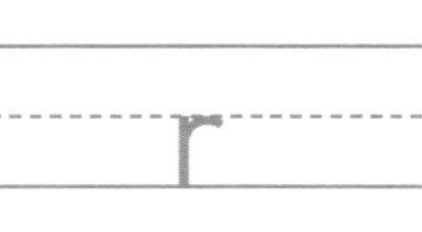 r

3 S    s

4 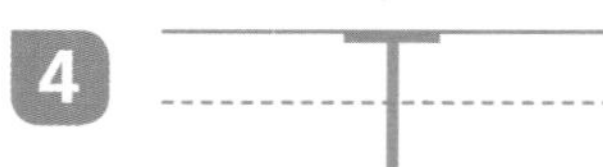 T   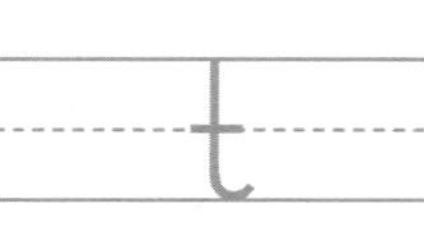 t

5  U   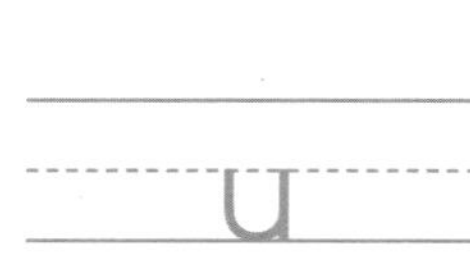 u

B. Match and trace.

1 T • •  • • 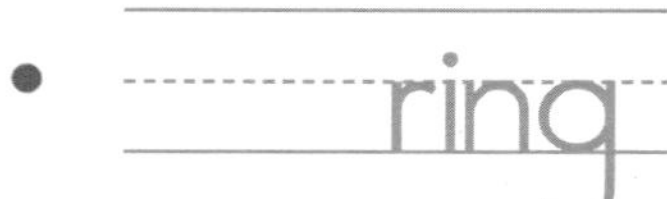 ring

2 R • •  • • 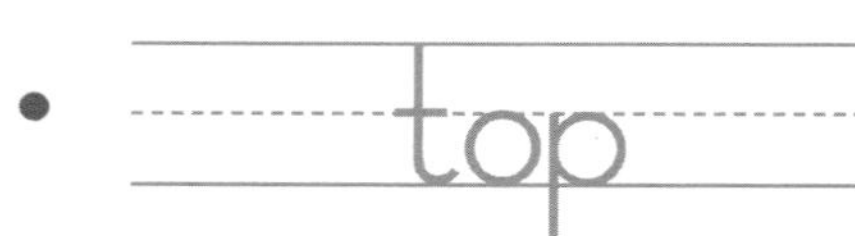 top

3 Q • •  • •  queen

4 U • •  • • umbrella

5 S • •  • • seal

C. Read and check.

1 A: Are you hungry?
B: Yes, I am.

 ☐  ☐

2 A: I like doughnuts.
B: Me, too.

 ☐  ☐

3 A: Do you like cookies?
B: Yes, I do.

 ☐  ☐

4 A: Do you want some hot chocolate?
B: No, thank you.

 ☐  ☐

D. Match and trace.

 • • No, thank you.

 • • I like candies.

3  • • Do you like cookies?

4  • • Do you want some yogurt?

Numbers

A. Trace and choose.

1 ⓐ Hi. Good to meet you.

ⓑ This is my brother, Bob.

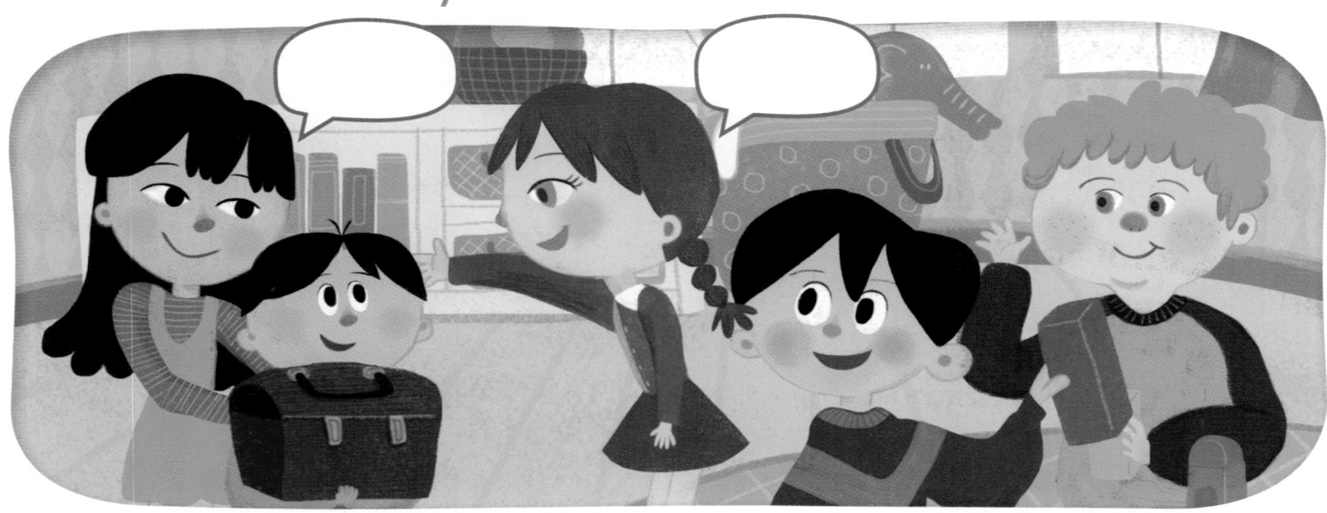

2 ⓐ Let's count.

ⓑ One, two, three, four, five.

B. Read and check.

1

- ◯ I like cookies.
- ◯ This is my brother, Tom.

2

- ◯ Here you are.
- ◯ Hi. Good to meet you.

C. Color, match, and trace.

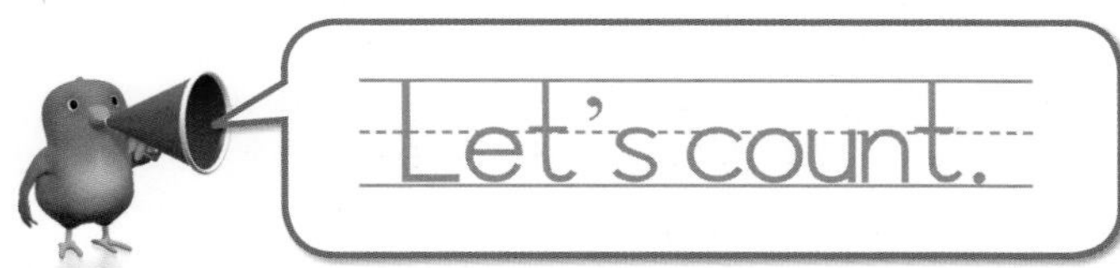

1	3	■■■□□	•	• One.
2	5	△△△△△	•	• Two.
3	4	○○○○○	•	• Three.
4	2	☆☆☆☆☆	•	• Four.
5	1	◇◇◇◇◇	•	• Five.

Lesson 18

Counting

A. Trace and choose.

1 a Goodbye.

b See you later.

2 a Three.

b How many birds?

B. Read and choose O or X.

1

Goodbye.

O X

2

See you later.

O X

C. Trace and match.

1. How many birds? •

2. How many dogs? •

3. How many rabbits? •

4. How many cats? •

• 

• 

• 

• 

Lesson 19 Alphabet Phonics Vv~Zz

A. Match and trace.

1   

2   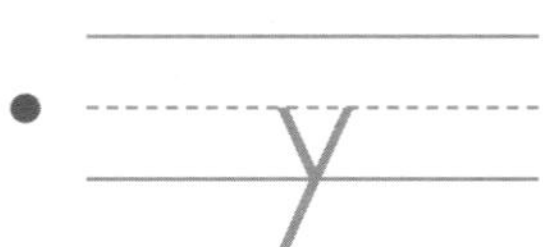

3   

4   

5 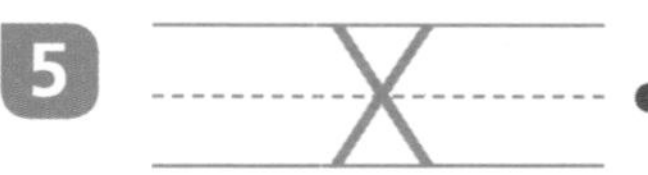  

B. Find and circle.

1   
r s e e g o x z o o d k t

2  
m i o v e t y a k o r h o

3 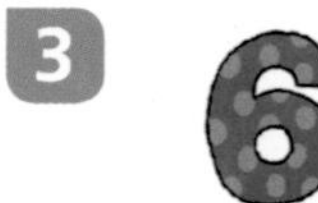 
s m a n u r s i x e h o x

4  
m a n o o u t y a k m o

5 
w o e d i s l t j w a t e r

Step Up 6

Lessons 17~18 Review

C. Read and choose O or X.

A: This is my brother.
B: Hi. Good to meet you.

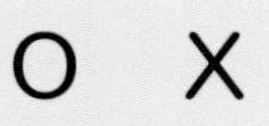

2

A: How many rabbits?
B: Four.

3

A: See you later.
B: Goodbye.

4

A: Let's count.
B: One, two, three.

D. Check and trace.

1

- ☐ How many cats?
- ☐ How many birds?

2

- ☐ Let's count.
- ☐ Three dogs.

Let's count.

3

- ☐ No, thanks.
- ☐ See you later.

4

- ☐ I like candies.
- ☐ Good to meet you.

Good to meet you.

Memo

ENGLiSH TOWN STARTER

ENGLiSH TOWN STARTER BOOK 1

English Town is a spoken English course comprised of a series of 9 books, specifically designed for elementary school students.

- Learning English in a communicative way and in an easy manner
- Focused approach to new words, expressions, and dialogs
- Fun to sing and chant together
- Simple but effective games and activities
- Exciting stories

Components

- Student Book
- Workbook
- Final Test
- Teacher's Guide including teaching resources
- Online (www.ybmenglishtown.com)
  Interactive e-book for teachers and students
  E-learning for self-study

www.ybmenglishtown.com

YBM

Final Test
English Town Starter Book 1

Class	Name	Score
		/20

Part 1 - Listening

[1-2] Listen and choose the beginning sound of the picture.

1  ① ② ③ ④ ⑤

2  ① ② ③ ④ ⑤

[3-4] Listen and choose the right picture.

3 ①  ②  ③ 

④  ⑤ 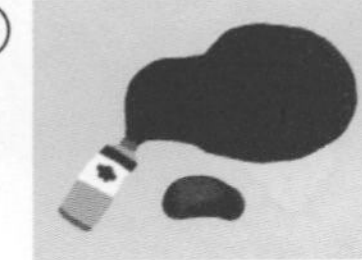

4 ①  ②  ③ 

④  ⑤ 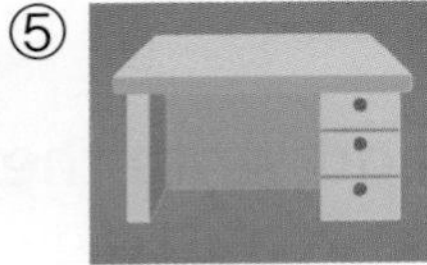

[5-6] Listen and choose the right sentence for the picture.

5  ① ② ③ ④ ⑤

6  ① ② ③ ④ ⑤

[7-8] Listen and choose the right picture.

7 ①  ②  ③ 

④ ⑤ 

8 ①  ②  ③ 

④ 

⑤

[9-10] Listen and choose the right conversation for the picture.

9  ① ② ③  ④  ⑤

10  ① ② ③ ④ ⑤

Part 2 - Speaking

11 Listen and choose the correct conversation.

① ② ③ ④ ⑤

12 Listen and choose the best response.

① I'm Tom. ② It's yellow.
③ Not so good. ④ Yes, it is.
⑤ It's a heart.

Final Test_English Town Starter Book 1

Part 3 - Reading

13 Read and choose the right word.

> **A:** I like candies. I like chocolate.
> **B:** ________, too.

① I ② Me ③ He
④ She ⑤ You

14 Read and choose the right answer.

> **A:** How many rabbits?
> **B:** ________________

① Sure. ② Five. ③ Good.
④ I'm Kate. ⑤ It's a bat.

[15-16] Read and answer the questions.

> **A:** Do you like doughnuts?
> **B:** Yes, I do.
> **A:** Here ________ are.
> **B:** Thank you.

15 What is the right word for the blank?

① I ② he ③ they
④ she ⑤ you

16 What does **B** like?

①  ②  ③ 

④  ⑤ 

[17-18] Read and answer the questions.

> **A:** Is it a window?
> **B:** Yes, it is.
> **A:** What ________ is it?
> **B:** It's an oval.

17 What is the right word for the blank?

① some ② many ③ shape
④ color ⑤ sorry

18 Which window is the right shape?

①  ② 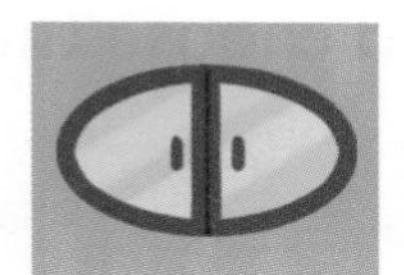 ③ 

④   ⑤ 

Part 4 - Writing

[19-20] Choose and write the right words.

green	traffic	some	red

19 A: What color is the ________ light?
B: It's ________. Stop!

20 A: Do you want ________ orange juice?
B: No, thank you.

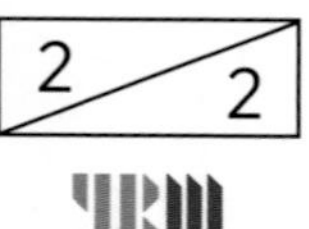